My SEVENTH MONSOON

T0346329

'What an encouraging and thoughtful book! It gives us on every page the reminder that our seasons are in God's hands. Not only this, but the book shows very clearly Naomi's evident trust at all times, not only for herself but also for her family, that whatever happens in our lives we may be quite sure God is in control. Then there is a clear pointing to the seasons God brings into our lives, all of which have a purpose. Her use of the passage from Ecclesiastes brings great encouragement to all our hearts. So much of her life in Nepal brings a clear picture of that lovely land and its people. The description of the patients she met in hospital is almost unbelievable to those of us who live in the West. Take time to read this book. You will be helped and encouraged.'

Jean Raddon
Founder of 'Know Your Bible' (KYB) ministries worldwide and an original member of the first medical missionary team to go into Nepal in 1952 (later to become the International Nepal Fellowship)

My SEVENTH MONSOON

A Himalayan Journey of Faith and Mission

Naomi Reed

Authentic

26 25 24 23   9 8 7 6 5

First published 2007 by Ark House Press
This revised edition printed 2011 by Authentic Media Limited
PO Box 6326, Bletchley, Milton Keynes, MK1 9GG
www.authenticmedia.co.uk

Reprinted 2012, 2017, 2022, 2023

British Library Cataloguing in Publication Data
A catalogue record for this book is available from the British Library
ISBN 978-1-86024-828-3

Cover design by Paul Airy at DesignLeft (www.designleft.co.uk)
Cover photos by Darren Reed and Maurice Lee. Used by permission
Internal photos by Naomi Reed, Diane Turner, Sandra Boone, Ali Wilkinson
and International Nepal Fellowship. Used by permission
Printed in Great Britain by Ashford Colour Press, Unit 600, Fareham Reach,
Fareham Road, Gosport, Hants., PO13 0FW

Contents

For Darren, Stephen, Chris and Jeremy.
And for all those who have shared a season with me
– because in doing so, you have added to my life.

There is a time for everything,
and a season for every activity under heaven:
a time to be born and a time to die,
a time to plant and a time to uproot,
a time to kill and a time to heal,
a time to tear down and a time to build,
a time to weep and a time to laugh,
a time to mourn and a time to dance,
a time to scatter stones and a time to gather them,
a time to embrace and a time to refrain,
a time to search and a time to give up,
a time to keep and a time to throw away,
a time to tear and a time to mend,
a time to be silent and a time to speak,
a time to love and a time to hate,
a time for war and a time for peace.
What does the worker gain from his toil?
I have seen the burden God has laid on men.
He has made everything beautiful in its time.
He has also set eternity in the hearts of men;
yet they cannot fathom what God has done from beginning to
    end.

(Ecclesiastes 3:1–11)

INTRODUCTION

It's a season . . .

It's July in Nepal and we're living in Dhulikhel, a traditional Newari town, set high on a ridge and overlooking the entire Langtang range of the Himalayas. Our house is halfway up one of the forested hills, on the outskirts of town. On a clear day we can see Everest from the top of the hill.

But today is anything but clear. July in Nepal means rain. It means solid, non-stop bucketing down rain. The streets have turned to rivers, the mud is knee-deep, the rice terraces are flooded and thick grey clouds have covered the Himalayas. As soon as I turn my back on something, mould grows. Every item of clothing that the boys own is either soaking wet or caked with mud. This is our seventh monsoon and I wonder whether we'll make it through. I wonder whether we'll cope with another 120 days of rain. I look out through the streaming window and try to imagine dryness. And I begin to long for another season.

But as I watch the clouds, I'm reminded that seasons don't move on until they're ready to. They move on in time, but only when everything is ready. And we look forward to that moment. Right now, in Sydney, the frost will be blanketing the gardens. Trees will be standing bare and bulbs will be dormant, waiting for their turn to add grace to the day. At exactly the right moment, though, the season will transform. Spring will come and bring blossoms and beauty. It will be a time to plant, before the summer sun dries up the ground. Right now, in Nepal, the monsoon is drenching the paddy fields but in time the clouds will roll away, the rice will be harvested and there will be celebration across the country.

Every season comes to a close and ushers in the next one. And it seems to be the same in our lives. A time of pain and suffering does eventually move on. Joys and blessings once again bring a thankful heart. A period of isolation or loneliness is replaced by an overload of human relationships. Confusion may come and stay for a very long time. But the next season is always close at hand.

Spiritually, perhaps, we also move in seasons. We seem to bounce between times of great intimacy and closeness with God, to times of dryness. Like a ping-pong ball that would rather stay still, I long for intimacy all of the time. But I know in my heart that it's not going to be. The phone call that heralds fear, the diagnosis that brings grief, the material season that gives abundance . . . all of these seasons not only affect the world in front of me but they also, in a strange and parallel way, affect my relationship with God.

So I peer into the fog and the clouds of my current season and I wonder what I'll gain from my toil. I wonder whether I'll see God's hand transform my seasons into beauty. And I wonder whether I'll ever fathom what he's doing from beginning to end.

1

A SEASON OF PREPARATION
Sydney, Australia

A time to be born . . .

Minimalism, adventure, frugality. Those are the words I would choose to describe my childhood. Both Mum and Dad came from good German and Scottish stock. 'Life wasn't meant to be easy.' 'Don't throw anything out.' 'That'll see you through another year.'

We had home-made clothes (and rucksacks and sleeping bags), no treat till we ate all our dinner, and no ice-cream out unless it was a birthday. We lived in a small fibrocement house in a Sydney suburb on a quarter-acre block – with one dog, two cats, four hens, nine ducks and a turtle. And we had the best holidays ever.

I was the envy of my friends. While they were sitting comfortably at a beach in Avoca, we were in wild country. Dad was a well-known rock climber who had made some famous first ascents. Mum helped to run the only bush-walking club in Sydney for years. So we were never going to have a choice. We learnt to cross-country ski as soon as we could stay upright. And then we were off . . . into the gleaming yonder, the rolling hills of the Snowy Mountains. But we weren't just off for a comfortable day's outing, we were off for a gruelling week of adventure. Our heavily waxed skis found their path in the virgin snow as our backs adjusted to the weight of the rucksacks. A fully loaded rucksack meant that the slightest lean to the left or right during a snowplough left me and the load in a newly formed snow crater. The end result was much the same as an upside down beetle, with skis stuck to her feet, wildly trying to reassume a vaguely upright position.

Everyone said, 'It must be so much easier learning to ski as a kid, you're that much closer to the ground.' Actually, an upside down 7-year-old impersonating a beetle, is a great deal closer to the ground. But the fully loaded rucksacks became very useful. The day's skiing would come to an end near a carefully chosen clump of snow gums, the tent would emerge and be erected on the snow, followed by the little gas burner and the billy full of macaroni. My brother and I would find our favourite places to sit in the nearest snow gum, and drink our cups of melted snow. The sun would be setting over the snowy horizon by the time the macaroni was ready and then, if it was really cold, we could curl up in our sleeping bags as we ate, gazing out of the tent window at the colours on the snow.

It didn't matter whether we were freezing in a blizzard on top of a mountain in New Zealand, trekking though the National Parks of Tasmania or liloing down a canyon in the Blue Mountains, it was the tent that was the constant companion, the refuge from the elements. On one wintry night, the thin nylon walls kept wild pigs from entering and demolishing our left-over macaroni. Their grunts came closer and closer, their shadows loomed larger than life, but the tent kept us safe.

There were so many stories to tell. But if you'd asked me about them then, you wouldn't have discovered very much at all. My third grade teacher certainly didn't. On one Monday morning she turned to me and asked me to share my weekend skiing adventure with the class for news. I sat there, mute and hopeless, pleading to be left alone and bypassed, in favour of those who could walk to the front of the room without wishing the floorboards would open up beneath them.

In the bush I could climb the cliff with the best of them, but in a social setting I peeked out occasionally from behind my mother's skirts. I fielded interactions from the safe confines of the blue and green cottons. The smooth gathers provided more than enough room for a small blonde head with her mouth closed.

One day a cousin said to me, 'You're very quiet, aren't you?' I looked at her. She had a strange necklace on. It had weird bones sticking out at all angles. I watched the way the bones moved as she breathed in and out. I tried to make up an answer to her question. I could have agreed with her, 'Yes, I am very quiet.' It was true, but it wasn't the entire truth. 'Actually, I think I'm very noisy inside my head. It just never makes it as far as my throat.' But as I thought about my reply, I couldn't bring myself to say it . . . and she moved away, in search of someone else to have a conversation with.

It was true. In those days my head was noisy, but it was also very unsure. I was unsure of everything: who I was, what I was like, what I thought about life. Even if my thoughts did make it as far as my throat, that wouldn't guarantee that they'd be interesting to anyone else. So it was much safer not to risk it, to stay quiet and to listen – and with any luck, people wouldn't notice me anyway.

I made my first real friend in high school. She had plaits right down to her bottom. But that wasn't the most surprising thing. By the time we'd made our way from English in Room 4 to Art in the loft, I realised what it was – she seemed to know who she was. She even seemed to be happy with who she was.

She kept inviting me to the Inter-School Christian Fellowship (ISCF), so of course I went. I went everywhere she went. And it was good! A hundred kids would pack into the music room every Friday, the guitars would come out and we'd be off. A hundred voices to the tune of 'From the rising of the sun . . .' It was a weekly fix of singing, praying and listening to the most ardent speakers we could find.

We found a good number of them. There's something about high school Christian groups that can radar an ardent speaker from about a hundred kilometres away. But, of course, all these years later I only remember one of them. And one of them was enough. As I melted into the crowd in the second row, he took the microphone and explained that God loved us, just as we were.

Apparently, God didn't love us 'just as we would like to be', but just as we were. It was the first thing that got me. I sat up and stared. Then he said that God had made each of us for a purpose that couldn't be fulfilled by anyone else on the planet. There was nobody else who could do it, not even the most talented people that I could think of – not even my cousin with her strange bead necklace. Then he shared one last thing. He said that God had loved us enough to send his only son to die for us, to die for me. And that meant that he must love *me, just as I was*, shy and quiet and hardly noticeable. The God of the universe had not only noticed me, he'd redeemed me and somehow made me acceptable. He delighted in me and had a purpose for my life. The God of the universe!

My 12-year-old mind was quietly astounded. Moments passed. Songs were sung and prayers were prayed. Other feet shuffled. Mine stayed still. The clock on the wall signalled the end of lunch. Bags were gathered and sandwiches stashed away. Bodies around me headed off to the next maths lesson. But I stayed where I was until the music teacher began making polite noises nearby. I had to stand up. And as I did, I knew that I'd somehow crossed over the line. I'd said yes to God. I believed in him. I'd said thank you.

It wasn't the most remarkable conversion. The beginnings of faith very often aren't. But it changed my life. I noticed, bit by bit, that the weight of other people's opinions felt less burdensome. I ploughed my way through the New Testament and any other Christian book that I could get my hands on.

None of my family went to church, nor anyone else I knew really. So for the first four years it was just God and me . . . and ISCF. But it was wonderful. I'd do it all over again if I could. And then, as I kept reading the New Testament, I began to see the challenge of the gospel.

> My command is this: Love each other as I have loved you. (John 15:12)

Even at 12 years old, I had an abiding sense that it wasn't enough to know the incredible love of God merely for my own comfort. If that was all it was, then I could go and buy myself a woolly blanket, or another sleeping bag. If God had really touched me, then it had to be about more than my own needs. If his love had really changed me, then that love had to be redirected outwards. 'Love each other as I have loved you,' he said. And the more I thought about it, the more I wanted to love others like that. But I wondered if it was possible. How many times does a 12-year-old get to lay down her life for another? I wondered what the commandment looked like on a day-to-day level.

A time to dance . . .

Then came 1984. That was the year I bumped into Darren on the dance floor of our school disco. And when I say bumped, I literally mean bumped. It must have been the music and the strobe lighting, because it took me a moment to figure out who he was. But only a moment. We were an item even before he had time to put his coke down.

My mother was not particularly impressed. She would look at me quietly as if all was well but her frown would give the game

away before the words began. 'You're still very young you know
. . . so try not to get too carried away. I just don't want to see you
getting hurt.' I agreed with her but I was too busy being carried
away. 'You could even play the field for a bit,' she said.

'But I'm not interested in the field. I'm interested in Darren.'
To me it was simple. If you happen to bump into the person
you were made and meant for when you're 15, then that's
when you bump into him.

In lots of ways we grew up together. He lived in the same
suburb and together we settled into the local church. It was a
great deal easier to do with a friend. And there was so much
more to learn of God and to understand about his ways. There
were church camps to go on, seminars to attend, songs to learn
and, very occasionally, another ardent speaker. Unbeknown to
them, every one of them would come up against my own
internal dialogue, the ongoing question: 'How can I love
others as God has loved me?' I'd listen to each of them very
carefully, looking for clues.

Meanwhile, Darren and I finished high school and went off
and studied physiotherapy together. Our parents became a bit
suspicious at that stage. They wanted to know who had actually made the decision to do it and who was tagging along for
the ride. There are still times when it's quite appropriate to
keep your mouth closed. We didn't tell them.

A time to embrace . . .

On a starlit night at the end of a jetty in 1989, Darren asked
me to marry him. I said yes, over and over again and quite
loudly, just to make sure he heard. He did. By this time we had
both landed jobs in the same physiotherapy department at a
big Sydney hospital. My friends thought it was a bit much.
Not only had we spent the last part of high school together,

we'd then spent three and a half years studying together and now we were going to work together. 'Don't you ever get sick of each other?' they asked.

'Well . . . no,' was the honest reply.

The following year, on a beautiful spring day, we were married. The azaleas were at that point where they blossom so much that you can't see the leaves. I felt like I was blossoming as well. I laughed so much that my face ached. Then we hopped on a plane bound for the Cook Islands. We flew in at sunrise and watched the way the pink glow touched the coconut trees. It couldn't have been more perfect.

When we're in a season of preparation, we usually don't recognise it. We certainly don't define it as such – and how can we? We're too busy living. We don't know what's around the corner. I didn't know then that my minimalist childhood would stand me in good stead for the years to come in Asia. I didn't know then that my childhood adventures were a prelude to the Himalayan ones. I didn't know then that my high school sweetheart was also being prepared for his life's calling. I just didn't know. None of us can know the ways we're being prepared for the future. But we can be sure of one thing – everything that happens in this season right now is part of God's bigger picture, part of the next season.

A time to search . . .

'Have you ever thought about serving overseas?' I asked Darren mildly. We were sitting on a grassy headland on the south coast of Australia, watching the waves crash onto the beach. A flock of seagulls were distractedly making their way to higher ground.

My question must have come out of the blue for him. He turned his head and paused before he replied. 'No, never. Why would I want to do that?' Then he thought some more. 'I'm happy here. I've got everything I could ever want. I've got you, my squash, a great job in a sports practice, all our friends at church, my family, everything. No way.'

The breeze was picking up and he began fiddling with his sleeves. I shivered and returned my gaze to the darkening sky. It was October 1991. We'd been married for a year and we were on another camping holiday. The tent was erected by the windswept beach and the billy was on the boil. I'd picked up a few of Helen Roseveare's books in a second-hand store to use as holiday reading material. And that was the first time that I saw in words what it might mean to truly love someone, 'as I have loved you'. Helen had spent 20 years in the Democratic Republic of Congo as a medical missionary with WEC International. Five of those months were in captivity during the revolution of 1964. Her books were alive with the challenge of missions and the enduring provision of God. As I read them, I became aware that the challenge was a bit too great.

What was I willing to do for God? I asked myself. (Only the easy stuff.) Where was I willing to go? (Somewhere close by.) In what ways was I putting limitations on the things I would or wouldn't do for him? (In a great many ways.) Did I really understand the extent of what he'd done for me, through Jesus? (Probably not.) What was the depth of my response? (Not as deep as it could be . . .)

I quickly told God all about my skin problems and my allergies and that I couldn't actually live in a hot climate. It's quite true. My skin comes out in bright red bumps if I'm in prolonged heat and sunshine. Sunscreen makes it worse and so does perspiration. It's an all over thing but it's especially bad on my face. It can be quite limiting even in a Sydney summer.

But in my hasty response I forgot that God already knew about me . . . that he'd made me like that. I read on. The next page of the book was all about his enabling and his strength in our weakness. 'My grace is sufficient for you, for my power is made perfect in weakness' (2 Cor. 12:9). Perhaps it's only in our weakness and our dependence that he can display his unusual power and grace.

So I had to come up with my next excuse. I reminded God that we weren't all that useful. We weren't teachers or nurses or doctors. We were physios and I'd never heard of the mission field needing physios. I expected the excuse to keep the churning at bay for some time. It did. It lasted a whole week and then I attended an amputee/ prosthetics conference in Melbourne.

I was sitting there happily listening to all the new and remarkable prosthetic advances coming out of North America. I was very comfortable; I was fascinated. It fitted perfectly with my line of work. I was heavily into improving the outcome measures in our amputee rehabilitation department. All sorts of new ideas were flittering around in my head – the things we could do at work once I got home.

And then it happened – the defining moment. Perhaps every life has one, in some form or another. At the time it can feel clean and sharp, drawing a line straight down the middle of the page so that everything that went before will forever be distinct from everything that comes after.

'These are the needs in Cambodia and indeed the whole Third World.' The doctor had taken the stage quietly. He showed a video which described the effects of landmines; the hundreds, if not thousands of amputees in that country even without crutches, let alone the hope of a prosthetic limb. There were no wheelchairs in sight either. He described the great need for physios in those places.

I noticed the head in front of me and the way my plastic chair felt out of place on the blue carpet. And I noticed that I no longer seemed to fit in the room either. In an instant I'd stopped caring about Cadcam sockets and hydraulic knees and outcome measures. What did it really matter if the patient took 3 weeks or 3.4 weeks to progress to a temporary prosthesis? What about the young man in Cambodia, hopping over a grassy bank to reach his bamboo house? What was his outcome measure? Did he have one? The contrast played around and around in my head.

Then, along with the questions, came the words of Jesus. They'd never seemed so strong: 'Love each other as I have loved you.' I sat there on the plastic chair in Melbourne and knew that I had my answer. The command to love others has to extend further than to my friends in Sydney. It has to extend to Cambodia and to the neediest places of the world because that's how far God's love extends. That's the reason he died.

I just couldn't help myself with Darren. He heard about the video over and over again and you can imagine his response. He wasn't particularly impressed. He was still talking about his life that had everything, and in a way he was right. Nobody in their right mind would want to change a life such as he had. But finally (to get some peace?), he agreed that he would seriously pray about it and leave me to follow up on any leads that I thought I had. It was just a gentle knocking on some doors, telling God that maybe we could go.

An answer to prayer

We knocked and prayed for about six months. Saying it like that makes it sound simple but in actual fact I had no idea where to begin. Our church wasn't particularly mission orientated. They supported some projects in inner-city Sydney but they hadn't sent cross-cultural workers overseas before. They didn't have links with mission agencies and I didn't know anyone else involved in mission.

So I thought I might as well start by getting in touch with the contacts I'd made at the amputee conference. After all, the doctor from Cambodia had clearly stated the need for physios. Did he have a need for us? I sent off a letter and waited. Weeks went by and there was no reply. Perhaps the letter got lost? I sent off a second letter but again, there was nothing. A few fruitless phone calls and I was again back to the drawing board.

When all else fails there's always the telephone directory. There was no Internet in those days. Surprisingly, though, there's quite a good list of mission agencies in the telephone directory. I decided simply to begin at the top and work my way down to the bottom. I had this little spiel going and I got quite good at it: 'Hi,' I said and then a slight pause while I tried to sound friendly. 'My name's Naomi and my husband and I are physios working in Sydney. We're Christians interested in using our gifts in the Third World. Would your mission be able to use us in any way?' I thought it was simple. The receptionists didn't seem to.

'I don't think so.' They said. 'We'll get back to you. And tell me again, what does a physio do?'

Then there were the agencies that required a three-year theological degree before they would consider us. In 1992, that just sounded way too long. We were keen to be out there! So down the directory I went. CMS, Interserve, OMF, SIM, Tear Fund, TLM. I was running out of options as I approached W.

But then I rang WEC and they said they could use physios in Gambia or Nepal. I put the phone down calmly and went to find Darren who was out the back cleaning our car. He lifted up the cloth, met my eyes over the shining chrome and knew straight away. We were going. We *knew* we were going to Nepal. Never mind Gambia. It was Nepal. The fact that Darren was just as convinced as I was became one of the most amazing parts. All of a sudden we were in agreement. Darren talks a great deal about the way God changed his heart in that instant. From then on he became the driving force.

But don't get me wrong. We're very ordinary people. We don't always feel that level of conviction. But that day we knew we were meant to be in Nepal. Of Nepal itself we knew very little. It seemed to be near India and have claim to the tallest mountains in the world. That was about all we knew. But we were convinced that God was going to send us there.

Unfortunately, the WEC fellow went on holiday and so my next phone call was again met with frustration. But the next day, a friend popped over for coffee and brought with him some Christian magazines for us to read. I still remember the moment I turned the page to see a double-page spread on the work of physiotherapy in leprosy. The work was based in Pokhara, Nepal. At the end of the article was the name of the mission organization: The International Nepal Fellowship (INF).

We'd never heard of them. They weren't in the telephone directory. But I knew we were going to Nepal, so I had to call them. And the voice on the other end of the phone didn't need clarity as to the role of a physiotherapist. 'Well, that's funny,' she said, 'I sent out an urgent advertisement for two physio-therapists yesterday.'

'It's us!' I cried. I think I forgot to put the phone down.

Darren was, at that moment, treating a patient in the physio practice nearby. In my excitement I rushed down to the practice and called him into the tearoom to tell him the news. Now, he's not given to public displays of emotion so he seemed to take it all pretty calmly. He acknowledged that it sounded pretty good and then he returned to the cubicle where his patient was waiting.

The patient turned out to be a local minister with a sore back. So in between mobilising his spine, Darren asked him if he'd ever sent any cross-cultural workers from his church. He thought for a while. 'Well, yes,' he replied, 'but we've only sent one. He works in Nepal with the INF.'

At that time there were only four Australians working in Nepal with the INF. But there we were, March 1992, an ordinary day in Sydney, having just found an article on physio in Nepal, INF, two physio jobs and the only other Sydney INFer all within half an hour. We could hardly say 'no'. We could hardly not go.

The months after that sped by rather alarmingly. We applied to and were accepted by the INF for a three-year term at Western Regional Hospital, Pokhara, Nepal. During the application process we found out some more about the INF. They were a non-denominational Christian mission that had been serving the people of Nepal since 1952. Being primarily a medical mission, they supported government hospitals, ran community health programmes and assisted with leprosy and tuberculosis control across the country. At that time, INF was composed of about 180 expatriate workers who came from fifteen different countries. They worked closely with the Nepal government to serve the people of Nepal and they supported the indigenous Nepali church.

We also found out more about Nepal itself. In those days it was classified as one of the ten poorest countries in the world. The health system struggled to support the larger cities, let alone the majority of hill communities. For a population that was then 20 million, Nepal had two Nepali bachelor-level physiotherapists. And one of those physiotherapists was apparently in the UK.

'That leaves one very busy physiotherapist,' we would say to each other, hardly able to believe that it could even be possible.

Then we attended Sydney Missionary Bible College and did an intensive missions course at UTC (United Theological College which is part of the Uniting Church in Australia). By then it was January 1993 and it was wonderful to spend time with a large group of people who were about to depart to various parts of the Pacific as soon as the course finished.

The problem was that we weren't planning to go to Nepal until the September of that year because there wasn't a language and orientation course available in Nepal until that time. And as the days wore on in January, we became more and more frustrated by that. The other twenty people that surrounded us couldn't stop talking about their new lives . . . but we still had eight months of 'normal' life to go. It was starting to become unbearable.

One afternoon we were walking through Parramatta Park on our way home from the missions course. I remember the canopy of green trees above us, the winding path marked by flowers and the manicured grounds stretching out on either side of us. It was a beautiful summer's evening and normally we would have enjoyed the beauty and the romance. But we hardly noticed it, let alone enjoyed it. All we wanted to do was to get on the aeroplane.

We tried to pray . . . 'Lord, you know us. You know that we long to serve you . . . and to get there. We know that you have good plans for us . . . but it's just so frustrating! If only we could go right now . . . but you must know what's going on. You must have a good plan or a reason for the wait. It must be to do with preparation. So, Lord, whatever it is, use these next eight months for your glory. Help us to be content with your plan and to stop running ahead with our own. Teach us your ways again we pray.'

It wasn't that we didn't have anything to do in Sydney in the meantime. We both still had good jobs. Darren was in the same private practice. I was now in charge of the rehab section of physiotherapy at Westmead Hospital, looking at outcome measures. We were also very involved in our church, running a Bible study and youth camps. Perhaps we were a bit too busy. But what we really wanted was that God would use the coming eight months in the best way possible to prepare us for our work in Nepal. And we had little idea just how perfectly he would do that.

2

A SEASON OF INADEQUACY
Khammam, India

The very next morning, right out of the blue, the season turned. It was actually one of those mornings that don't start off too well. First of all, the alarm didn't go off, so we were running late for our missions course, then we mislaid the car keys and struggled to get out the door. But we made it just in time and as soon as we put our bags down, we were approached by the head of World Mission, UCA.

'I'm not sure whether you'll be interested in what I have to say,' he said. 'But last night I had a phone call from the Church of South India. They have an urgent need for physiotherapy help in their Polio Home and mission hospital in Khammam, South India. The only problem is that the maximum visa you could get is six months.'

This man had no idea what we were planning. He had no idea of our timing to head to Nepal. We looked at each other and smiled, feeling sure it was right. It was as if as soon as we put our hearts right again, God placed the last piece of the puzzle in our laps. Six months was the exact time we had available. And surely being in Asia amongst the poorest of the poor would be the best training ground possible. So we said yes as quickly as we could, without asking any questions and both trying hard not to look too excited!

Then all of a sudden we were leaving the country in less than six weeks. We panicked. I wrote out lists and lists of things to do. There were so many things to do that it was easy to forget the important things. One thing that we failed to do well was to raise support money. It was partly due to INF's policy at the time which meant that being a 'faith' mission we weren't encouraged to bring up the issue of money with potential supporters. If anyone asked us what our needs were, we were allowed to answer. But if no one brought it up, we were to stay quiet. Well, the funny thing was that not many people brought it up! But, fortunately for us, God had a plan and he raised up an amazing group of people from our church, as well as various INF and wider connections around the state, and we always had just the required amount. Not a cent more, not a cent less. Years later we discovered that one of our dearest prayer warriors came out of retirement purely for us. God gave her a part-time job and she put her entire earnings into our support costs. What a humbling realisation.

We did better at raising up prayer support. INF has various prayer groups that run in Sydney and have met faithfully to pray for Nepal for the last thirty years. It was an honour and privilege to attend these before we left. I think up until that point we hadn't caught a glimpse of the wider work of God in our country. We'd become very involved in our own church but very little beyond that, so all of a sudden we were being exposed to mission on a much wider level. We met people who'd served in Nepal since the country opened to the outside world back in 1952 and we stopped in our tracks to listen to their stories. That was another humbling experience. We realised that we were just a very, very small part in God's big plan and feeling smaller all the time.

Finally it was time for the goodbyes. We held an all night worship session and invited everybody we knew. We must have stopped singing at some point but I don't remember it. Then the next day we found ourselves at Sydney airport, hauling our rucksacks onto the airport trolley and catching the last glimpses of our friends and our family and everything else in our world that was safe and familiar.

One way ticket

Aeroplane trips are great . . . the longer the better. We needed the whole twelve hours of flying time as well as transit in Bangkok to recover from the emotion of the airport scene. After a few hours in the aeroplane, I noticed that I was breathing normally again and I became engrossed in the in-flight movie. It wasn't particularly good but it was escapism at its best. I floated away to another land where beautiful people lived in big houses and owned fancy cars. And then it was over. The long list of credits was rolling and my eyes slowly moved away from the screen and took in the rows of sleeping bodies around us. And then I suddenly realised: I was not in our lounge room.

As the thought hovered in my mind, the screen abruptly told me exactly how far away from our lounge room we were. As if I wanted to know. Then it told us how quickly we were being hurtled into lands that had no connection with our lounge room: 800 kilometres per hour. That's fast. It struck me for the first time that we didn't have return tickets and that we were likely to be in Asia for at least four years. It seemed like forever. I was 24. Four years might as well be a lifetime.

I knew that I needed much more than escapism so I rummaged in my bag and opened a couple of remaining farewell cards that had been thrust into our hands at the airport. And I found what I was looking for. Someone had quoted from Psalm 139:9–10:

> If I rise on the wings of the dawn, if I settle on the far side of the
> sea, even there your hand will guide me, your right hand will

hold me fast.

I read the psalm, I looked at the card and then I looked out the window at the bleakness of the Indian Ocean. It seemed very deep and very dark. It could have swallowed up the entire scene from the in-flight movie. It added to my worries. Then I watched the Bay of Bengal as it appeared in the distance and seemed to steady it. The 'far side of the sea' was coming into view; the place where we would settle, the place where his hand would guide us and hold us fast. I sat still and enjoyed the thought for a moment. The pictures in my mind remained frightening but they no longer held me. The Almighty did.

After the transit in Kuala Lumpur, the mood on the plane changed dramatically. All of the other travellers now seemed to be of Indian origin. We could hear lots of different languages but none that we understood. The flight attendants started passing around disembarkation cards and, as soon as we'd filled in our own names, Indian faces started leaning over the seats and asking us to help them with their cards, crowding us from the aisles. They spoke to us in Hindi and Urdu and Bengali and Tamil . . . but in 1993 our untrained ears didn't pick any of that up. It just sounded like noise.

But we knew they wanted help and they assumed we could do it. They even began to throw their passports into our laps – unusual names and colours and details written in other languages. It was our very first moment of feeling inadequate. We looked at each other and shrugged, not even sure if we were meant to be laughing or not, certainly not able to do anything useful and momentarily worried by that.

Then we were both straining out the window, our eyes glued to the scene outside. The ground got closer and the patchwork network of paddy fields became clearer. Small specks became people working in the paddy fields. Men looking like ants were working on building sites, carrying dirt and concrete on their heads in small flat trays. Madras seemed to be full of strangely shaped white buildings. India! The sense of foreign unfamiliarity overwhelmed us and I started to wonder whether it might be better to stay on the plane.

The March heat was suffocating. The crowds at the airport mobbed us. Someone took my watch in the fray. How did that happen? I didn't feel a thing. Where were we meant to go? We had no way of even knowing who was meant to be collecting us, if anyone. All our cross-cultural training had taught us well: always carry essential phone numbers with you. We failed miserably there. All we could see was a sea of Indian faces and colourful saris clamouring for our business. Then we were weaving through traffic on a tiny motorised *tuk tuk*, dodging cows and bullock carts. Either side of the road, don't let that bother you. What are we doing here?

Recognising the season

Our time in India turned out to be the best training ground. We had no language, no other Westerners and no orientation. I couldn't put my sari on. Five metres of slippery nylon is just a bit too much of a good thing. I couldn't even make a cup of *chiya* without provoking laughter, let alone a proper curry. The first time I attempted a South Indian curry, our guest was not complimentary. He turned the food over in his mouth and considered whether to swallow it or not. Then he said, 'Well . . . if my mother had made this, I would have thrown it out the window.'

Restraining my desire to say something rude, or even throw the curry at him, I managed to recognise the season. It was a season of inadequacy in its sharpest form. I couldn't do the simplest of activities: dressing, cooking, talking, listening . . . I was hopelessly and utterly inadequate. I felt like a child, needing to learn everything from scratch again. I didn't even have scratch. It was an extremely difficult season.

We lived in a one-roomed 100-year-old 'house'. When the monsoon came, we discovered that it had twelve rather big holes in the roof. That meant that there was literally nowhere we could put the bed without getting rained on. But of course in 50-degree heat in South India we weren't complaining.

'But it's refreshing!' we kept saying as the stream of water from one of the larger holes found its course down our legs. We came to the unanimous conclusion that sleeping with rain pouring on your legs was much easier than sleeping with rain pouring on your head. That was after testing the various alternatives. There was a gas burner in one corner of the room and a toilet in the other. 'Pull the curtain across!' we would shout at each other if someone came to the door.

Running water was a thing of the past. The thing to do was to walk across a large bumpy field carrying an enormous flask on your shoulder, queue up with the other women, fill it up, and then carry it home. It sounds simple. Well, an hour later I arrived back in tears with precious little water in the flask, my *punjabi* completely drenched and my arms aching. Here was another thing that I couldn't do. The things that I couldn't do had easily overtaken the things that I could do. Actually, the things that I could do felt non-existent.

Going against all cultural norms, Darren took over the water-collecting role. The women that gathered at the tap decided he must be weird. They whispered and laughed and pointed at him from behind their sari folds. They were as fascinated as they were confounded. You would be hard-pressed to find an Indian man at the water tap.

But while they were busy being mystified, Darren was busy gaining new insights into the 'woman at the well' story. So that's why she was there at midday. Midday is a crazy time to collect water. The heat could melt you in a moment. Nobody is at the tap at midday. Actually nobody is anywhere in India at midday, it's siesta time. Now there is a lovely new habit to get into.

Khammam is a small town 200 kilometres east of Hyderabad. That also means that it was 200 kilometres away from the nearest toilet paper. When we arrived in March it was stiflingly hot, dry and dusty. Most of the town is flat with dirt roads connecting the bazaar to the rest of the town. The only real mode of transport is the cycle rickshaw. We would hail a cycle rickshaw at the hospital gates and make our way down to the bazaar. It sounds odd but it took us quite a few weeks till we recognised what was a shop and what wasn't a shop. 'Shops' were small box-like rooms with a shutter opening onto the dusty street. They would be filled with all manner of goods hidden away in boxes. At the beginning 'shopping' was pure guesswork. Having no idea what was hidden, how could we ask for it? Even if we did know what was hidden we wouldn't have been able to ask for it anyway.

A time to be silent . . .

We picked up some Telugu vocabulary (through necessity) but never gave it our full attention. We were 'saving' ourselves for Nepali. Darren did manage to get the bargaining thing down pat though. One afternoon he spent a good half-hour arguing with a rickshaw driver over the price of the return journey. Darren knew that 4 rupees (5 pence) was the acceptable rate and he was absolutely determined not to pay 5 rupees (7 pence).

Back at the hospital, we were inundated by all sorts of weird and wonderful conditions, as well as impossible requests. A lady brought her child who was deaf and dumb and asked us (the physios, with no Telugu language) to fix her. How could we do that? Another man brought in his bike tyre. What for? We had no idea. A young girl tried to give me her unwanted baby. I was even tempted to take it. Children with polio were brought from far afield, the parents having spent their last rupee on the journey. They would grovel on the ground kissing our sandaled feet, begging us to admit their children in the Polio Home. There is nothing nice about having grown adults grovelling in the dust trying to smother your smelly feet with kisses.

The desperation overwhelmed me. I couldn't get my head around the state of their lives. Sometimes it seemed easier not to try. We would go on home visits to assess the needs, along bumpy dirt roads and past endless acres of rice fields to a 'village'. The village consisted of a handful of mud huts and hammocks. Inside each hut was one hook and one piece of clothing, as well as some clay pots for food and water. I had never imagined such an absence of 'stuff', even with my minimalist upbringing. A young child with polio would crawl out on their bottom. There were no calipers, no crutches, no wheelchairs and no hope.

'Come to the Polio Home . . . you may walk,' said our fellow staff-members in Telugu. The families would look back at us dumbfounded. Could that really be possible?

We saw that it was possible at the Polio Home. One hundred children lived there permanently with schooling on site. Almost all of them had been found in derelict conditions in remote villages. They were provided with cheap calipers made on site and taught to walk with crutches. For the very first time they stood upright and could see over fences, reach door handles and talk to someone face to face. They discovered how tall they were. They discovered that they were, in fact, of worth. They were made in the image of God and he loved them . . . and so did the staff. The love changed them.

One week the children were busy making peanut butter and jam. It consumed them for days and then they enthusiastically tried to sell it to us. What's behind this new venture, I asked myself. Why are they so driven? It turned out that they wanted to support a little blind girl who was living at a hostel nearby. They needed 350 rupees per month to do it. It seemed impossible for children with nothing themselves. And we realised that week that there's nothing quite as humbling as generosity from those who have nothing themselves. If only we could learn some of that.

Meanwhile, we were learning quite a bit about the various parasites and giardia that were invading our intestines. Everyone expects to get sick in India. Without clean drinking water, it's virtually impossible to stay well. We had also known that, but were completely unprepared for the first bout. We must have thought we were dying because we even rang Sydney to get our prayer chain going. After that bout, we amused ourselves by seeing who could clock up the best record. I can't remember who managed the 30 times in 24 hours, but it was certainly a miserable state to be in.

At the same time, the mercury crept up to 52 degrees. No, really, 52 degrees Celsius! The locals also told us it was rather hot. We soaked towels and draped ourselves in them in order to walk the hundred metres from our room to the Polio Home. Without the dripping towels, the likelihood of passing out was probably greater than the likelihood of reaching our destination. We had a small fan in our room but the electricity seemed to be off more than it was on. A clay pot kept our water cool and that was about it for amenities.

But we also had a cobra. We found it near the toilet and our friendly neighbour quickly came to our assistance by chopping its head off. Going to sleep was even trickier after that particular episode. Slightly easier than the cobra in the toilet was the buffalo at the back door. I'm not sure who owned him but he was always poking his head in the door, looking for food. The first time I turned around and saw him there I got a real fright.

But he quickly turned into company. He must have decided he was on to a good thing because our back door was the officially designated place for everyone to throw their rubbish.

May is the hottest month in India. All the polio children went home for the month because it was too hot to do school. Business being slow, we also took the opportunity to travel south and try to cool down. As well as that, it was a good time to stop and reflect on what we were doing during this difficult season in India. Apart from feeling inadequate, we couldn't really think of a great deal. We weren't sure. There was certainly a need for physio, which we were fulfilling. It was a privilege and a blessing for us to spend time with the children. But we were such a long way away from our old lives and church involvement.

So often in life, we try to measure how we're doing. Not only do we do that, but we use as our yard stick a comparison with either someone else or some other season of our own lives and it usually makes us feel worse. And while I was doing exactly that, I began to realise that God doesn't deal in comparisons. He wants surrendered hearts. His work is to mould us and use us and it's OK if we feel helpless. It's OK if we feel inadequate because that's the way we are. Our work is simply to remain in him and trust that he'll do the rest. While we were away, we came across a passage in Habakkuk 3:17–19, which seemed to put it well:

> Though the fig-tree does not bud and there are no grapes on the vines, though the olive crop fails and the fields produce no food, though there are no sheep in the pen and no cattle in the stalls, yet I will rejoice in the LORD, I will be joyful in God my Saviour. The sovereign LORD is my strength; he makes my feet like the feet of a deer, he enables me to go on the heights.

To us, during those six months in India, it felt like there was no fruit on the vine. Not only were the living conditions extremely difficult, but we couldn't see any fruit of our presence there. Why indeed were we there? And why had we come there at such a rapid pace? We didn't know. But we learned that we didn't need to know. The important thing was to remember who we were living for and who we were rejoicing in and who was our strength – the Sovereign Lord.

Maybe that's the main thing we learn through seasons of inadequacy. We learn that we don't need to know everything and that's not a bad discovery. Maybe it's our 'adequacies' that cloud our vision during the ordinary seasons. Maybe they stop us from discovering *his* adequacies. They stop us from discovering that it's his strength that enables us 'to go on the heights'.

Something green

We arrived back in Khammam in June with a renewed vision and purpose. We would use any opportunities that came our way to love and pray for people. Beyond that, we would rejoice in God and in the place where he'd put us. The place where he'd put us cooled down. The rains came exactly on time on 13 June. It was our first monsoon. Dry dusty lanes were transformed into fertile green growth overnight. Where did all those plants come from? Where did all the colours come from? The dust that had been blinding us was no longer airborne. It was firmly rooted to the ground, in deep squelching tracks of mud. We were unsure if we were actually living in the same town.

Along with the rains came Munna. Munna was a nephew of our Indian Pastor and he'd just finished six months of physio technician training in South India. He was a gift from God for us. A committed Christian, he was probably the humblest man we met in India. He had a servant heart and a deep contentment. We spent the next three months working alongside him every day. Darren particularly enjoyed having someone else to work with. Munna not only translated all our Telugu problems but was also keen to learn as much as he could during those months.

In July we were also privileged to join some young Indian evangelists on trips to poorer villages where they were providing medical help and conducting church services for anyone who was interested. Everyone seemed interested! The headman of the village opposed the visits at first, but he accepted the medical help. His wife was interested in the new teaching and secretly attended the services. The man found out and made her life a misery. He drank heavily, was easily enraged and she struggled under the abuse. By the time we visited, he'd been opposing the visits for over a year and was ready to pull the plug on them. Then one night he had a dream and in the dream he was caught in a fire in his house, with no way to escape. Jesus came to him and told him that knowing God was the only way out, the only way to life. The headman gave his life to Jesus that same night. The visits continued and the whole village came to Christ.

Running ahead

The season was looking greener but I was still frighteningly aware of my helplessness. One day, a state minister and his army descended on the Polio Home to try to hand out oranges to the children. There were hundreds of oranges, boxes and boxes of them. For one scary moment they assumed that I was in charge of the whole show and would direct the distribution. If only I could say something of sense in Telugu, like, 'No, thanks, try asking Vigi. She's the one you want.' But I couldn't.

Expressing myself clearly has become one of my favourite things to do . . . even though it didn't used to be. In the season of preparation, my mouth was often shut. But I think that even in my wordless childhood, the words were still there. They were just turning themselves over in the wings, waiting for their turn on the stage. But now the hobby has become the words. I bounce them back and forth until they come back at me with some sort of freshness. Then I listen to other people's words and dissect them and analyse them until I get a feel for what's going on for them.

But in India I was illiterate and it was the hardest part of that season. I think my lack of words hurt more than the lack of water, the lack of electricity, the lack of toilet paper, the lack of health and the lack of friends. Not only could I not convey my thoughts well but I couldn't understand anyone else's thoughts well either. Maybe the only good thing to come out of it was my resolution – to throw myself into learning Nepali as soon as we crossed the border. I wanted my words back. And in many ways my mind was already in Nepal. I'd begun to count the days till we moved.

Do you ever find yourself doing that? Jumping ahead of yourself to the next season, well before you actually get there, usually to the detriment of the 'now'? I seem to struggle with this all the time. By nature, I see the possibilities and the potential around the next corner and I often can't wait to get there. So my mind goes running ahead, sometimes months ahead of my body. The problem is, of course, that the body that has been left behind fails to use all the wonderful opportunities that still surround it.

I must have been in that state at the end of our time in India. I remember giving myself a lecture every morning during our last month: 'Try to live fully where you are. Use the opportunities in front of you.' I did actually make an attempt to move more deliberately. I played in the sand with the younger children and I stopped to chat to the older children. I went to the bazaar to buy more balls and I prayed with my Indian friend who was the doctor at the mission hospital. I tried really hard to live for the moment and then the moments ran out. It was time to leave (amidst much Indian fanfare and farewells). We had muddled through. We had learnt more about grace than anything, more about helplessness and more about laughter amidst the sorrow.

3

A SEASON OF ADJUSTMENT
Pokhara, Nepal

Head to the hills

Any time spent on an Indian train is time well spent – just for the sheer full-blooded experience of it. There are three tiny shelves on either side of the cabin . . . for sleeping on. There's a squat loo in the next carriage which is in constant and dire need of an empty, never mind the ammonia. Then there's a continual stream of beggars who pile on at every stop in the desperate hope of a rupee or two. They reveal their mangled hands and missing digits to you and the foot-kissing thing starts again. 'Oh no,' you think – and you learn how to conceal your feet behind the nearest large object. Then you learn how to conceal your sense of guilt behind the nearest well-thought-out and appropriate justification.

The platforms are always filled with vendors shouting their wares. The smell of spices and curries floods the senses. The trip from Khammam to Calcutta takes 36 hours but there's so much going on that you forget to look at your watch. That is, if you still have a watch. At one point in the night we heard shouting coming from the next carriage and a neighbour went off to investigate. 'Oh, don't worry,' he said. 'A man just pushed another man off the train.' At full speed. Ohh . . .

The variety of Indian languages really only hit us on that train journey. As each hour went by, our companions changed and so did the language. They moved from one to another with little effort, depending on who spoke what. At one point, we were delighted to discover that one set of fellow travellers were Christians, so we all launched into a well-known hymn and then it went on in various languages. I never sing it now without thinking of that train journey.

I know not why God's wondrous grace
To me he hath made known,
Nor why, unworthy, Christ in love
Redeemed me for his own.

Refrain:
But I know whom I have believed,
And am persuaded that he is able
To keep that which I've committed
Unto him against that day.

I know not how this saving faith
To me he did impart,
Nor how believing in his Word
Wrought peace within my heart.

I know not how the Spirit moves,
Convincing men of sin,
Revealing Jesus through the Word,
Creating faith in him.

I know not what of good or ill
May be reserved for me,
Of weary ways or golden days
Before his face I see.
I know not when my Lord may come,
At night or noonday fair,

Nor if I walk the vale with him,
Or meet him in the air.[1]

There's so much that I don't know, I thought, more now than ever. But, I know whom I believe in and I trust him for the next journey and the next season, whatever it might bring.

I quite like finding myself momentarily in between seasons. It doesn't happen very often and, when it does, the moments are fleeting. Sometimes they're unrecognisable because the season is going to shift without warning. And even when they are recognisable, like on that train journey, I have to notice them and think quickly before the next season swamps me. So we spent some of that train trip writing down all the things we had learned in India. I felt like I'd become a different person to the one who had flown in only six months earlier. My worldview now included the women at the well and the unwanted babies, the foot-kissers and the persistent peddlers, the generous children and the village headmen. My understanding of God's faithfulness through every circumstance was now also firmly held. Well, maybe it was firmly held until the next trial loomed. We had begun to learn about culture and language, 'begun' being the operative word.

Relief

Flying into Kathmandu was an enormous relief. After the craziness of Calcutta, we were entering the Himalayas – and we could see them stretched out on either side of the aeroplane, gleaming white and unbelievably high. Bright green foothills seemed to leap up towards us and tiny farmhouses were dotted on every hillside. I thought about the twenty million people who lived in such a small kingdom, the size of Victoria, and I wondered how they fitted. Then we could see raging rivers cut into the valleys. Apparently, it had been a heavy monsoon that year and almost every road was cut, washed away by landslides. What else was washed away with it? I wondered. How many lives?

The aeroplane came in to land and we could see buildings up closer. Everything seemed unfinished. Were they going up or coming down? Some days later, a friend explained, 'No, that's just how they are.' Oh. There was no mobbing at Kathmandu airport. Instead, a friendly INF face appeared and ushered us into an old green van, which meant that there was also no haggling over taxi fares and nothing was stolen. Ahhh. We could do this. Compared to Calcutta, we could do anything.

The old green van took us to the INF flat where we recovered overnight before the ten-hour bus trip to Pokhara the next day. Pokhara lies 200 kilometres to the west of Kathmandu along the Mahendra Highway, which is the main highway linking the west of the country to the capital. Two hundred kilometres doesn't sound like much at all. You can cover that sort of distance in two hours in Australia. But in Nepal it takes ten hours. It might well be one of the country's best roads, but that doesn't mean that it's built for speed. It can't be. It's built straight through the middle hills of Nepal. On a bad day, I would say that it's built primarily for the purpose of motion sickness.

On our left, the 'hills' went straight up. We had to crane our heads out of the window to see the tops of them. On our right, and at least 30 metres below us, lay the Trisuli River. Like an untamed tiger it roared down the valley, taking hold of everything in its path. Around every second bend loomed another landslide, another pile of mud and boulders strewn straight across the road. Every now and again there was a cluster of Nepali workers, carrying the boulders away in the cane baskets on their backs. At this rate it will probably take them a year to fix one landslide, I thought to myself. Even years later, it still seems that way. Man pits himself against the elements, like ants against a runaway steamroller.

On that particular journey, our driver was clearly frustrated. He made up for the constant delays caused by the landslides by flying around every clear corner he could find. In some ways that added to the heart-stopping 'views'. It meant that as we were flung around each corner we could actually look straight out of the window and down into the Trisuli River. There was nothing at all between us and the river . . . except 30 metres.

We learnt that it was much better to look up. Eight thousand metres up on the other side of the river sat the Annapurna Himalayas. They spanned the entire horizon and loomed even larger as we drew closer to Pokhara. We wondered how large they were going to get? Perhaps if we took our eyes off them, they might disappear . . . much like an apparition or a movie set. But no, they stayed put, like an ancient immovable wall, a mighty fortress of snow and ice – the largest of all God's creations. We sat in awe.

Pokhara in those days had a population of about 100,000 people. The town itself stretches along a valley, which was fashioned by the *Seti Kola* (White River). At some points the river widens to become an inviting delta. At other points it snakes along inside a narrow gorge. At the very top of the valley and closer to the mountains was the setting for the INF headquarters and mission compound. In the middle of the valley is Mahendra Phul, the main bazaar area. Slightly further down is the Western Regional Hospital (WRH) and right at the base of the valley is INF's leprosy hospital (Green Pastures). Off to the left of the town is a tranquil lake bordered by tourist hotels and restaurants. From virtually every point in the town, a glance to the north reveals the entire Himalayan spectrum. To us, arriving straight from the flat plains of Southern India, it seemed like a perfectly delightful place to be.

A time to plant . . .

We settled ourselves into a little flat on the INF compound and began our three-month period of intensive language training. Having not had any in India, we lapped it up. After our classes finished for the day, we'd return to our room, light the candles and practise our conjugated verbs . . . usually incorrectly, but we still practised them. Four other families and three singles were in our language group. Charlie and Linda had arrived from the UK with their four children, aged three, five, seven and nine. We looked on in admiration as they attempted to settle the kids into the strange environment. Steve and Fiona had two. That was perhaps more manageable but definitely still impressive. Andrew was our age and up for adventure. He became our trekking partner and Friday night dinner guest for the next three years. There's nothing quite like being in a strange and foreign country together to form a lifelong friendship. But that was before the practical jokes started.

We celebrated our third wedding anniversary eating *dal bhat* in the local bazaar. We had one bicycle for the two of us, so I would sit side-saddle on the rack and Darren would pedal furiously. This particular night, the monsoon had again been heavy and the little streets were flooded. The *bijuli* (electricity) was off, as it was every night, either between 6 p.m. and 8 p.m. one night or 8 p.m. and 10 p.m. the next. The good thing about that was it always reminded you what day it was and what time it was. But this particular night we'd also forgotten our torch. So there we were, pedalling in pitch darkness through a maze of side streets, with water halfway up the wheels and unable to see a thing. Now that was fun! While we'd been busy romancing, however, Steve and Charlie had been busy digging an enormous pit, five metres to the left of our front door. A cryptic note detailing a treasure hunt would have led us straight into it. But we never could do cryptic crosswords. The pit still waits today.

One month into our language course we decided to move out of the INF compound and in with a Nepali family. We thought that there was nothing quite like exposure for language learning. So after the ease of the INF compound, we soon found ourselves living again in a tiny room, this time above the buffalo. When *Aama* (our Nepali mum) first showed us the house she pointed out the single tap that stood outside the building in full view of the house and numerous neighbours. I stayed quiet and watched for a while to see how the other women washed themselves. It took me a few days but I discovered that they either went early in the morning or late in the evening, they wrapped themselves in a *lungi* and did the whole shower thing under the cold tap. Now, I must tell you one important fact. By this time it was winter . . . winter in Nepal at the base of the Himalayas. Freezing!

'I can't do it,' I said matter-of-factly to Darren, who was quite understanding. He had figured out how to wash with the males of the household: in the middle of the day in bright sunshine! So the next trip to Mahendra Phul saw us bringing home a blue bucket. It did quite well with some warm water from the kitchen and if I was careful I didn't make too much of a mess in the bedroom. Actually, buckets are a very useful invention. The squat loo in this household was way down the back, past the rice fields. There was no lighting and there were masses of crawly creatures. That was all fine in the daytime, but dead scary at night. So we purchased a second blue bucket and I grew very fond of both of them.

A distinct lack of Weet-Bix

Traditionally, Nepali families eat two meals a day. The first one happens at 10 a.m. and the second one happens at 7 p.m. Both meals are exactly the same: a massively heaped plate of rice, lentil soup and often a vegetable curry, altogether known as *dal bhat*. If it's a special occasion they might also eat a chicken curry. In between times, Nepalis drink *chiya* which is a sweet milky tea drink. Now, we'd been eating curry for breakfast in India, but not every single morning. So during our initial days with *Aama*, we started to reminisce fondly about the Weet-Bix we'd left behind in Australia. But it wasn't long before we were hanging out for rice and curry in the mornings. And we definitely didn't want anything for lunch. In fact, we couldn't remember what it was that used to appeal about lunch.

In the kitchen in our new household, there was a small table and two chairs. *Ba* (Dad) was the prime occupier of the first chair. He hardly ever moved. Darren was extremely privileged to occupy the second chair. I sat on a very small stool on the floor and *Aama* hardly ever stopped moving in order to sit down anyway. But when she did, she sat on the floor. She worked from before sunrise to well into the night. She milked the buffalo, dug the fields, harvested the rice, cut the grass for the buffalo, made yoghurt and buttermilk from the buffalo milk, cooked for the family and tended the vegetables. She told us one morning that she married *Ba* when she was 8 years old and hadn't had a day off since then. That was in answer to my question about holidays. She'd already told us that she was 64 years old, so I stared at her uncomprehendingly as I tried to imagine working for fifty-six years without a break. Perhaps I hadn't heard her correctly, I thought. My Nepali must be even worse than I thought it was. But yes, that's what she said.

Her four daughters were all married with children, working equally tirelessly in their new households. Child marriage was made illegal in Nepal years ago and the age of marriage has risen over the years, particularly in the towns and amongst the educated. But in some villages it remains shockingly low. A recent study in the Bara district found that 98 per cent of children were married before they were 8 years old.[2]

One day, I was in the kitchen practising my conjugated verbs with *Aama*. She was sitting on the floor, making buttermilk by churning the buffalo milk in a clay jar. The jar twisted rhythmically as she pulled evenly on the two stout ropes. Her feet invisibly provided a steadying force. She'd been forging on in this position for a long time and the physio in me must have thought she needed a break. So I had a turn. It really does require some skill, particularly the invisible feet. If they don't do their job, the whole thing can tilt and buttermilk can spurt all over the room. The raining buttermilk can then drip down the backs of the only two chairs and filter through your hair. But I did eventually get the hang of it (sort of).

It struck me, though, as I sat there on the floor, hair congealing, how adaptable we are as humans. In some seasons we find that every detail of our lives has suddenly changed. It can be the food we eat, the surface we sleep on, the way we shower, the language we speak, the things we do for fun. A year earlier I would never have conceived of myself sleeping above the buffalo, showering in a bucket, eating *dal bhat* twice a day and churning buttermilk for fun. But that day it felt quite normal, almost unquestionably normal.

I guess the changes can be anything. The people we live with, the town we live in, the church we attend, the roles we assume, the friends we keep. The backdrop changes and we find ourselves in a season of adjustment. Often, the adjustments are large and they take our time and energy. Sometimes it feels like it's taking *all* of our energy and we don't have anything left over. Maybe the thing to remember is that we do eventually get there. At some point we end up looking back and realising that we've crossed over the 'normal' line. We don't even know when we did it but imperceptibly, ever so slowly, life has taken on its new shape and become the new season. We don't even recall what 'normal' is any more or indeed if there ever was one.

A new home

Before we knew it, our months of language were over and it was time to get on with real life. We needed to remember why we'd come and we needed to find a house. That was the first thing. But it proved more complicated than we expected. In Australia, you pick up the Saturday paper and turn happily to the 'For Rent' section. Then you ring the estate agent and, before you know it, you've moved in. In Nepal, there was no such thing as advertisements in the local paper or estate agents or any other signs of properties for rent. 'But what does everybody else do?' we kept asking.

'Well, it's like this,' replied an old and experienced friend. 'You sort of just wander around the streets and fields. If you see a house that you like, you kind of poke around, knock on the door and maybe try to find out who lives there. If you find the owner, that's great. If you don't, you might find someone else who knows the owner or knows where they might be. Maybe they'll be overseas. But sooner or later you might find them. Then you kind of just chat and find out if the owner would like to rent it to you. Sometimes all the family will move out and let you live there. Sometimes they won't. So then you keep walking until you find something else you might like.'

'Ahhh,' we said, pretending to understand. 'That could be fun.' And it was fun. There's nothing I like better than wandering around streets and fields and trying to imagine living in the little houses. And as we walked around the streets and fields of Pokhara, there were endless possibilities for imagining. Finding landlords proved far more difficult, though, and fulfilling INF's criteria (for fly screens) and our criteria (no high fences) was even trickier. It took so long that we ended up house-sitting for three months until we found something that worked. But it did work.

The house was made of stone and concrete and painted yellow. A low stone wall bordered the garden (patch of overgrown grass) and on the other side of the wall lived two enormous snortling pigs. Through every window was a framed picture of the 8,000-metre Himalayas. Inside the house there were two small bedrooms, a living area and a kitchen. The squat toilet was out the back, but it wasn't so far out that I would need a bucket. There was apparently a water problem. Everyone said to us, 'You won't cope without water.' But we thought to ourselves, 'We've lived in India; we'll cope with anything (well, kind of).' There was a tiny gas stove, no fridge, no microwave, no washing machine, no hot water, no telephone, no vacuum cleaner and no transport. But it was much, much better than a tent.

At the hospital

In order for us to work in Nepal, only one of us needed the official work visa. So Darren took the post of Physiotherapist at Western Regional Hospital (WRH), Pokhara. I didn't really put up too much of a fight – especially when I saw what his work entailed. His adjustments at work became a story in themselves and I can't really finish this chapter without including them.

Darren began work at WRH in December 1993. He entered the season with a fair amount of trepidation. During our years of work in Sydney he had quickly settled into the life of a private physiotherapy clinic. He spent his days treating lots of sports injuries and some chronic backs as well. If you gave him a footballer's knee he was in his element. But footballers' knees were few and far between in those years in Nepal. There wasn't even a little one.

In those years, WRH was a government-run 200-bed hospital. It had been built in 1978 as the successor to the Shining Hospital, which had been an INF-run project. A regional hospital, it serviced at least three million people in the western district. Many patients came to the hospital after having walked for a week through the surrounding middle hills. Those not up to the journey would be carried in a cane *doko* (basket) on the back of an obliging (and strong) relative. About ten other expatriate INFers also worked there in those days, all under Nepali leadership. Charlie, an anaesthetist, and Andrew, a dentist, were amongst the ten. Their stories during the season of adjustment kept us entertained around dinner tables for the next three years. The physiotherapy department consisted of a few plinths that served the outpatients, some plaster of Paris, an ultrasound, and some pulleys. And they were all sitting smack bang under the maternity ward toilets.

My own experience of the maternity ward toilets was to come later. But suffice to say that they're always full and when squat toilets are full they overflow all over the floor. Every now and again, the cleaning staff would get fed up with it and grab for the nearest long object and start attacking the toilet, in the cheerful hope that the more they poked the more it would all eventually disappear. Well, they were right. Disappear it did. On one of Darren's early days in the physio department, he was distracted by some loud poking noises coming from directly overhead.

'Is everything OK up there?' he queried.

'Oh, that's fine, that will just be the maternity ward toilets being cleaned,' replied Bijay happily. Bijay had worked in the department for sixteen years as the official 'on the job' trained physiotherapist. If Bijay hadn't seen it, no one had seen it. So that day they went back to the job at hand which was plastering a young girl's fractured forearm. More plaster, more warm water and more reassuring chat with the mother. Then the sound above became louder and the ceiling started to make a suspicious rumbling sound. Not long after that the drips started . . . just a few, nothing to worry about.

'We need to get this girl's plaster finished,' said Bijay. With both hands engaged in the plaster they couldn't move anyway. Then it came in spurts, a heady mix of blood and faeces . . . all over the room, in every direction you could see. With a sound like an explosion, the dedicated cleaner had managed to push his way all through the pipes and the floor. He had indeed caused the mess to disappear. It now covered the entire physio department and Darren and Bijay, not to mention the little girl in her new forearm plaster.

With that auspicious beginning to his Nepali physio career over, Darren merely had to turn his attention to wards full of conditions that he'd never seen before. As in any Nepali hospital, the medical wards were full to overflowing with dysentery cases, tuberculosis, tetanus, typhoid, snake bites, as well as a few strokes and head injuries. The orthopaedic wards showed the more usual upper and lower limb fractures. The causes of the injuries were stories in themselves, though. Most of them had been sustained whilst cutting grass with a sickle. But it wasn't the sickle that did the damage. It was the height from which they fell.

Many Nepalis keep a buffalo or a few goats to milk and if they can sell the milk, so much the better. They usually keep them under the mud house, just like *Aama*. But there's no grass to eat under a mud house so the women then spend up to six hours a day cutting grass to feed the buffalo. It's quite remarkable how much one buffalo can eat in a day. And with more of

Pokhara becoming urbanised, the the women have to go further afield to cut the grass. Grass cutters typically find themselves hanging over high cliffs to reach some more prolific grass or plucking fresh leaves from the top of a very spindly tree, which also hangs over the cliff. Hence the broken limbs.

The other busy place in the hospital was the burns ward. In Nepali mud homes, the open fire is most often in the centre of the house. Mum cooks around it; everyone eats *dal bhat* around it; and then they curl up on bamboo mats to sleep around it. In chilly winters, it makes sense and the children get the most central spots of course. But this then means that they can end up rolling into the fire during the night. During the three years that Darren worked at WRH he saw more than 300 acute burns cases and about 80 per cent of those were women and children. Another causal factor of burns is kerosene stoves and long, flowing nylon saris. It's not a good combination. But, indeed, burns are a hospital feature the world over. A more problematic feature in Nepal was the number of post-burns contractures that were seen in those years. To come to a regional hospital is a very big deal for Nepalis. They need to consider what's happening in the fields and who will harvest the rice if they leave at a critical time. Can they afford the journey? Is a family member available to carry them there? Is it actually worth it?

Even once they're at the hospital, the problems aren't over. Due to the severe shortage of nursing staff, patients also need a family member to stay with them, cook their meals, wash the bed linen, and sometimes even change the dressings. The impact on the farming community is great. So, very often, families will either decide not to bring the patient or will wait till after the rice season, when life becomes more manageable. If a patient survives the original burn but doesn't receive medical intervention, the chance of a post-burn contracture developing is very high.

The burns patient usually keeps the limb in the most comfortable position and that tends to be with the limb flexed. Skin always sticks to skin. One little girl who had a serious burn under her knee sat curled up in a corner for months. Her entire posterior thigh stuck to her posterior calf until her heel was attached to her bottom. It wasn't a very functional position. This little girl's father eventually brought her to hospital and, fortunately, a skin release operation and masses of physio soon had her walking again. Another girl was burnt under her chin in such a way that her chin ended up sticking to her chest wall. She couldn't turn her head or even close her mouth in order to chew and swallow. Again, an operation and a physio splint had her eating and talking once again. But it's not always a happy ending.

A 7-year-old boy presented with his entire left arm stuck to his chest wall. An operation was available but the family refused. They couldn't afford the time. In the end, the family makes the decision and we need to learn from them. We need to listen to their issues and the wider implications. We need to adjust to their way of thinking. But it's still hard to walk away or to watch the patient walk away.

Not only were nurses in short supply, so wore other vital products. Gloves, dressings, bandages, water, even blood. That was a much trickier issue. In most hospitals in Nepal there's no such thing as a blood bank. If a patient needs a blood transfusion the relatives must find someone with a blood match and then donate the blood themselves.

Mukti was a 20-year-old lad who came from a village two hours' walk to the north of Pokhara. He had been carrying a long steel pole and had run into some electrical wires. The severe electrical burn had left him with both arms amputated below his elbows and a major burn on his buttocks. He was losing blood quickly and would soon die without a blood transfusion. He had no relatives with him. The friend who had accompanied him from the village was trying to make himself scarce. Darren somehow found him, then sat with him for a long time to try to reason with him . . . calmly. Why on earth wouldn't he help his friend?

Well, it was a long story. It turns out that Hindu Nepalis generally refuse to give blood. They believe that in giving blood they lose some of their spirit. It's too great a risk.

'Yes, but your friend will die any minute now.' Darren said. 'Look, what if I come with you and sit next to you, what if we both give blood together? Will you do it then?'

Still not convinced, the friend merely agreed to walk with Darren to pathology. But that was a step in the right direction. Once they were settled in pathology, Darren claimed his advantage, 'All right. I'll do it first. You watch. Then you do it.'

Very carefully, as the bright red blood entered and filled the syringe, the friend studied Darren's face. He watched for any ill effects or departing spirits. The blood continued to make its journey and the friend looked even more closely at Darren's face. Eventually he decided that he couldn't see any spirits, so he hesitated for a few more moments and then agreed to give blood for his friend. Just in time.

Mukti survived. Some weeks later, Mukti questioned Darren as to where the blood came from.

'Well, your friend gave blood,' Darren replied.

'Really! He would never do that! He would be too scared. He did it for me?'

'He did. He saved your life,' Darren paused. 'I also gave blood.'

Mukti stared. 'You gave blood? You gave blood for me? You don't even know me!'

'That's true. But there's one thing even more amazing than that. You've received blood from us and your life has been saved. In fact, your name *Mukti* means salvation, in Nepali. But the one who has really saved your life is Jesus. He shed his blood for you and he saved not only your physical body but your entire life. He saved you so that you could live forever with God, even after your life here runs out.'

Mukti had never heard of such a person as Jesus. He wanted to know more and he wanted to know why Jesus loved him. Then he wanted to know if he could know that love for himself. Some days later he gave him his life on that hospital bed. He had no hands – but he had one life. The last we heard Mukti was starting a fellowship group back in his village.

To change your religion in Nepal is a serious thing. In those days, Nepal was the only Hindu kingdom in the world and had a population of over 80 per cent Hindus. The rest were either Buddhists or Muslims with some tribal beliefs thrown in as well. The first Nepali Christians began an indigenous church in 1952. It has always been Nepali-led and governed and over the decades the numbers have grown to what is today a thriving national church, with a particular heart for evangelism. Following along later came a desire for the church to be involved in social action and community issues.

Over the years, INF members have been involved in the local Nepali church at a very behind-the-scenes level. Our agreement with the government states that we will not openly evangelise, but will continue to practise our faith personally and at a one-on-one level, as conversations arise. In a country that is not our own and in a language which is not our own, that, of course, is just perfect. Sometimes it feels that God is doing such a great work around us that we merely look on in wonder, learning to trust in his wisdom, his plan and his outworking. That, too, can be an adjustment.

Maili was one such instance. She was a 35-year-old lady who lived in a village some days west of Pokhara. She struggled to eke out an existence in a small mud hut and her husband had a great fondness for the local rice wine. Her three daughters arrived in rapid succession and her husband was not impressed with that. He needed a son to perform his funeral rites in order to gain entry to the next life, so he threatened Maili that he would take another wife if she couldn't bear him a son. One day it all became too much for Maili. She doused her body with kerosene and set herself alight, managing to give herself second and third degree burns to 60 per cent of her body. But she was still alive.

It was in this state that Maili arrived at WRH emergency department. Darren met her on the ward some days later. It was clear that she didn't have long to live. A few days passed and her condition deteriorated. She was being given painkillers as she waited to die. On this particular day, Guru Aama was in the next ward. She was a devout Nepali Christian and would regularly visit the hospital to talk to the patients. She was small and wiry and more than 80 years old. Her husband had been one of the first Nepali pastors. This particular day, she was looking for another patient so she stopped Darren and asked him if he knew where that patient was. He didn't. Guru Aama started walking slowly away when a single thought popped into Darren's head.

'Guru Aama!' he called as she began to leave the ward. 'I know someone who wants to talk with you though.' Actually he didn't, but he had to get her attention somehow. 'It's the lady with the severe burns over by the window.'

Guru Aama went and sat quietly by Maili's bed. As soon as Maili laid her tired eyes on Guru Aama, she became animated. She couldn't lie still any more. As they started to talk, a remarkable story unfolded.

'Last night I had a dream,' said Maili slowly. 'I dreamt I was walking along a high Nepali path that kept circling the cliffs. It was a thin path I didn't recognise. I was carrying such a heavy *doko* full of great burdens and all my worldly possessions. It weighed me down and I couldn't continue.

So I stopped at a fork in the path and sat down on a large rock. I looked at the paths ahead and there were only two. One path went up over the cliffs; the other path went down. I had no idea which way to go, so I sat and waited. As I waited, a lady came to speak with me. She was small and she had grey hair tied up in a bun. She sat down near me and she asked me which way I wanted to go, whether I wanted to go up or down. I wasn't sure. I couldn't tell. And then while I was still wondering, I woke up, not knowing what the dream meant . . . Then this morning you came to my bed and you're the lady in my dream. I know that it was you.'

Guru Aama smiled at her. 'My dear girl, I could ask you that same question. Jesus is the only way to God. He loves you. He wants to know which way you will go. He says he will take you on the path that leads to life. He will carry your burdens for you and give you peace. That's what he came to this world for. He came for you.'

Maili had never heard of Jesus before. She asked to hear more and then, that morning, she gave her life to the Lord. She died the next day, at peace, her burden lifted.

God has indeed got a plan for each soul – a plan that only he can work out. And what do we do? We look on in wonder at a God of the individual, a God who cares deeply and unreservedly for each one that he created, a God who will not let them go.

Maili's last request was for her family. 'Please tell my mother and all my family and everyone I know about Jesus. They don't know about him yet.'

Language blunders

Passing across the 'normal' line in a new season can indeed take a long time and perhaps it takes longer in a work environment where we arrive with certain expectations of 'the way things are done'. But the season of adjustment has some built-in bonuses – entertainment being the major one, for us as well as the onlookers.

The very best way to stay humble as an adult is to attempt to learn a new language and then actually try to use it functionally. Language blunders at work not only keep you on your toes but they also provide massive entertainment value for those hovering around to check out what dumb thing the *bideshi* (foreigner) is going to say next. It's quite easy to send the nurse off to get some bandages (*potti*) and then to spot her coming back with a candle (*botti*), no doubt wondering what on earth the strange white physio wants that for . . . especially in the middle of the day. We should be saving candles for the next power cut. But it's another thing when you're actually trying to communicate something of importance to the patient.

Teaching exercises to patients is the staple diet of the physiotherapist. If you can't teach doable effective exercises to a patient, you can't do anything. And it turns out to be even more important in Nepal when a patient's 'length of stay' is next to nothing. They're on their way (usually on the relative's back) before you've remembered their name and bed position. You would think that exercises could even be taught with a moderate amount of gesticulating and hand waving. But no, the more you gesticulate, the more potential for finding yourself in a pickle.

One day, Darren was trying to get a young man, post hip fracture, out of bed for the first time. Also on the patient's bed happened to be sitting five of his friends and relatives. Darren wasn't even sure that they all belonged to that patient. They could well have been from the next ward but, with a keen sense that something more interesting was going on here, they had slowly gravitated. Darren started off with a simple command to the patient: '*Ubhinos* (Please stand up).'

All five men stood up. All five men, that is, except the one he wanted to stand up who was still lying on the bed. Looking straight in the eyes of the patient, Darren tried again, '*Ubhinos*,' he said.

All five men stood up again. Darren smiled and decided he needed to try something else. Maybe he would look at the patient's leg.

'*Tapaiko khutta kumchaunos* (Try bending your knee).'

All five men started vigorously bending their knees, in perfect unison with each other. It could have been synchronized swimming, except that the patient himself was happily unaware that he was meant to be doing anything. Darren then produced the crutches and demonstrated their use. He put them in the patient's hands. All five men jumped into action and, heaving the patient off his feet, carried him round the bed. The problem was that in their enthusiasm, the patient didn't actually come anywhere near to weight bearing on the ground. It could have gone on like that for another few hours. On countless other occasions, Darren explained the exercises the patient must do, only to find that the relative had spent the next week doing them daily.

'Not you!' he would say. 'The *birami* (patient)!'

4

A SEASON OF ENRICHMENT
Pokhara, Nepal

Green Pastures

While Darren was adjusting himself to the peculiarities of a government-run general hospital, I had the much easier task of settling in at the INF-run leprosy hospital, Green Pastures (GP). It was more than easy. It was enriching. It even became an enriching season. For starters, many more of the staff spoke English. Secondly, I really only had one condition to become familiar with: leprosy.

Leprosy is a mildly contagious disease spread by bacteria in nasal droplets. It affects the superficial nerves of the forearm, lower leg and face. Nerve palsies are common. Lack of sensation and movement contribute to recurring injuries and ulcers, particularly in the hands and feet. In those years in the hospital there were three very experienced Nepali physio technicians who did an excellent job treating the pre- and post-op tendon transfers as well as the neuropathic foot ulcers.

Even in Nepal in the nineties there was a great deal of stigma attached to the leprosy diagnosis. Our INF mobile teams regularly found patients hidden away, living alone in the caves, having been cast out from the villages. Once a patient begins multi-drug therapy, they are no longer contagious. But unless the general public becomes aware of that fact, the stigma will live on.

Green Pastures was the only leprosy treatment facility in the western region of Nepal, so patients would come from many days' journey. Actually arriving at GP and finding the attention they desperately needed was life-changing for thousands of them. One young man told me, 'No one has ever loved me until now. Now, all I have to do is walk in through those doors and I'm loved.'

The man's name was Shankar. He had grown up in a village six hours' walk from Pokhara. When he was an infant, his mother had disappeared with another man and that left his father to care for the young family. A combination of malnutrition and tuberculosis took their toll and, when Shankar was eight, his father died. At the same time the telltale signs of leprosy started appearing on Shankar's arms. Up until then the children had been a burden on the village but now they were downright unwanted. They were refused shelter and food and then banished from the village. How does an 8-year-old live without food? Not very well.

Shankar's story would have ended there. But right on cue, a villager heard that there was a place called Green Pastures in Pokhara that would give treatment to people with leprosy. So Shankar and his 10-year-old brother set off by themselves to this unknown place. They had no money and they had no idea of what lay ahead.

It was a life-changing journey. Shankar had never seen a road. He'd never seen a moving vehicle, let alone been on one. He'd never seen the brightness of an electric light or noticed the way it eerily casts out shadows in the evening. The light drew him – like a moth to a flame – to the gates of Green Pastures. He stepped across the cattle grid and knew that he'd come to a place of acceptance; a place where people are valued because they're made in the image of God, not because they're without blemish. He experienced love and acceptance for the first time and his young heart responded eagerly. He filled his empty stomach with good food and he filled his empty soul with the words of Jesus and the love of his fellow man. He flourished. He learnt to read and write and was encouraged to do further study. He grew in contentment.

When we first met him, Shankar was back working at GP, teaching other young patients to read and write. He lived in a tiny room not far from the hospital. There was one hook on the wall which held his change of clothes, and there was one wooden bench in the corner where he slept. 'Look at all this!' he said to Darren. Darren slowly looked around the empty room. 'I've been so blessed!' said Shankar. 'God has been good to me and I'm full of thanks. You know, I'm even thankful for my leprosy because if I'd never had leprosy, I'd never have known Jesus and I'd never have known how much he loved me.'

Every Tuesday morning at GP there would be a time of Bible study and fellowship for any of the patients who were interested. It was held in a little room off the medical wards and the patients would trickle in, shuffling their feet a little, take a seat on tiny stools and look at the floor. The leader was Chandra. He'd also been a victim of leprosy but he now worked full time at the hospital. He would lead a few Nepali worship songs and then pick up his worn black Bible.

One Tuesday morning he said, 'Today we're going to read from a book at the end of the Bible. It's about what's going to happen . . . and this is what it says . . .' Chandra started reading slowly from Revelation 21:1–4:

> Then I saw a new heaven and a new earth, for the first heaven and the first earth had passed away, and there was no longer any sea. I saw the Holy City, the new Jerusalem, coming down out of heaven from God, prepared as a bride beautifully dressed for her husband. And I heard a loud voice from the throne saying, 'Now the dwelling of God is with men, and he

will live with them. They will be his people, and God himself will be with them and be their God. He will wipe every tear from their eyes. There will be no more death or mourning or crying or pain, for the old order of things has passed away.

There was quiet in the room for a while and some of the patients started slowly raising their stumps of hands and staring at them. Others looked down at their feet, which were so deformed, covered with ulcers and open sores. They started to cry. All they'd ever known was that they were nothing, they were the outcasts, the untouchables – they didn't even deserve food. And now suddenly this – hope for an eternity with God where there would be no more tears. And then they held their hands even higher and it was as if they were trying to imagine being made new, with whole hands and restored feet. And more of them were crying and others were singing and I was as well. In that moment it seemed as life-changing for me as it was for them because I, too, needed to understand hope from the position of the hopeless, to believe in Jesus, from the position of the untouchable.

It was perhaps one of the most moving Bible studies I'd ever been part of and, for months afterwards, all I wanted to do was to read the Bible as they read it, to imagine what that would mean. And as I did, I longed more and more for the day when we'll all be a part of that great multitude from every nation, tribe, people and language, standing before the throne, falling on our faces and singing praise song after praise song to the God who is going to wipe away every single tear.

Imagine! Our voices are going to join with Chandra's and Shankar's and Maili's and Mukti's. Our eyes will meet theirs and we'll be together forever in that place where he's going to make all things new, even our rotting hands and hearts. And we'll be on our faces before him, the one who never once forgot us, even in our caves, far, far away. He never so much as took his eyes from us, let alone gave up on his plan. Sometimes when we sit comfortably in Western churches we forget. We don't fully see that God is at work on every mountainside, on every hill, in every cave and desert plain. His eyes are on those he loves, drawing them back into a relationship with him.

The World Health Organization had a major focus on leprosy during the nineties. They aimed to eradicate the disease worldwide by the year 2000. But case detection was always going to be tricky in Nepal, a country with 20 million people, massive Himalayas and very few roads. How could they find the cases in order to eradicate them? Even mobile clinics only seemed to skim the surface. Education programmes by radio began to reach those who were reachable but word of mouth (especially of cure) had the greatest effect.

But even once they found the cases and cured them of their bacteria, would that be the end of the task? Unfortunately not. At GP, patients came by the droves who had successfully halted the spread of the bacteria, but who had seriously deformed hands and feet as a result of the nerve palsy. Nerves don't regenerate, and neglected nerve palsies lead to further injury and further damage. All of those patients had great need of reconstructive surgery and physio in order to have functioning hands and feet again.

So I spent the next year trying to gauge the level of disability or impairment in our referral area. I went on mobile clinic trips and reviewed the records of 1,082 cases. I crunched numbers on the computer and one year later came up with my conclusion. Forty-four per cent of 'cured' leprosy cases had significant ongoing rehabilitation needs after their 'cure'.[3] It's not enough in the field of leprosy to 'cure' patients. A worldwide emphasis (and funding) needs to go into care after cure. Happily, in the next twelve years, GP became a specialised rehabilitation centre and did exactly that.

Outside Green Pastures

Whilst working in Australia I'd done a few home visits. You pick up the keys to the hospital Commodore, put a few walking aids in the ample boot space, turn on the air-conditioning, the FM radio, and ten minutes later you're there, in downtown Westmead. You check you have the correct address, greet the patient, assess the walking needs and then hand out the appropriate gait aid. It's quite simple.

Home visits in Nepal were anything but simple. My first home visit was to see Josh Maya who was a 60-year-old lady with bilateral lower limb amputations. She had lost her right leg below the knee and her left leg above the knee. At Green Pastures, the prosthetic department was ably run by Hari. Sarah, an English prosthetist, was consultant and creative deviser of anything new. She had become fed up with using old, hand-me-down, Western above-knee prosthetics and decided that they would create an above-knee prosthesis in Nepal using only cheap locally available parts.[4] That meant she used old pieces of piping, bicycle axles and even film canisters to provide suction. It worked brilliantly and Sarah's first client was young and strong and quickly proved the design to be a great success. Her second client was Josh Maya.

Now, whenever you're interviewing a client and discussing potential prosthetics, a major part of the chat revolves around the social history of the client. Where do you live? How far from the road? What's the house like? Where would you be walking? How far would you walk and would your relatives help you? Where's the toilet? These questions were always very easy to ask from the safe (and level) confines of the GP hospital. But even when the clients answered that in fact they lived on the side of a cliff and, yes, it was very steep, I still didn't quite get it. I couldn't quite picture it. So, because this was a complicated case, we decided we needed to do a home visit to check out the usefulness of prosthetics in her particular setting. So the next week, Sarah, Darren (who came as our porter and chief guide) and I set out on a rickety Nepali bus heading south-west out of the Pokhara Valley.

The road wound around a swollen river, past landslides, terraces of rice, unending hills and switchbacks. Three hours later, with spinning heads, we alighted and proceeded to follow Josh Maya's instructions to find her village. She had described it as being an easy two-hour walk up a few hills. An easy two hours later we were nowhere near her village. We were far, far from it. We had enjoyed numerous stops for further instructions and *chiya*, all the while provoking much interest on the part of the villagers. They'd never seen a white face before so the news travelled on ahead of us: 'The ghosts are coming! The ghosts are coming!' One whole school of students emptied the building and surrounded us to stare and touch our skin. There's no hiding as a *bideshi* in Nepal.

An elderly gentleman passed us on the path and casually inquired where we were going. 'To visit a friend,' Darren replied. Oddly, after that a whole bunch of his companions stared at me most peculiarly as they passed me on the trail. At our next break we realised that Darren had actually said that he was 'going to sell his wife'. A simple mistake in Nepali where *bechnu* (sell) and *bhetnu* (visit) can oh, so easily become muddled. Luckily, we had no takers.

The path continued to take us further upward and around huge terraced cliffs dotted with simple mud dwellings. Six hours later, as dusk approached, we climbed the last mountain and could see Josh Maya's 'village'. Half a dozen mud huts sat on the edge of a cliff. Literally, four or five metres in front of her hut was the cliff. A rocky path connected the houses to our trail. There was no way that path would be traversable by a bilateral amputee. It was hardly traversable by us. We couldn't even imagine the toilet situation.

We were lavishly greeted by all the family. We took our time with the greetings (no more wife selling), then removed our shoes and bent double in order to creep into the darkened mud room. Josh Maya sat on the floor by the fire, which was in the middle of the mud room. She was busy cooking a feast of dried out chicken and rice to honour us with. I wondered worriedly what they would eat for the next month. There was nothing else in the room, except smoke. The smoke was getting in our eyes and ears, and it was becoming difficult to see. It appeared that Josh Maya sat on two small cane mats. She would lever her bottom from one to the other in order to stir the pots on the fire.

We made our way back outside to breathe again and discuss our options.

'She wants to walk. She thinks she can.'

'But where on earth is she going to walk?'

'There's about three metres here.'

'It's still exercise.'

'Theoretically.'

In the end, the relatives decided she should have the chance. They brought Josh Maya back to hospital the following week in a *doko*. That was after we had also safely returned. We'd spent the night above the buffalo and then made our slow descent back down the mountain to the road-head. We then shared the roof of a bus with thirty Nepalis and a dozen goats that spent the greater part of our journey dropping little black pellets on our laps. It was a far cry from the air-conditioned Commodore, but once back at GP I had a renewed vision. I certainly had a clearer picture of life beyond the hospital. If nothing else, I could now put my fertile imagination to work. If a patient described his village as a bit hilly, a bit of an incline, I now thought 'edge of a cliff'.

Adding to our ordinary pictures can be an enriching

process. It can be part of a very enriching season, particularly if we choose to see it that way. We begin to see beyond what we thought was there and sometimes a lot further beyond. The 'Aha!' thing happens over and over again, until we think there are no more 'ahas' left in us. In a similar sort of way, adding to our ordinary definitions can be a part of the enriching season. I found that out with worship. My definition of worship back in Sydney was nothing like what it became in Pokhara. I hadn't learnt the secret yet.

In church

A five-minute walk down our lane brought us to Nepali church. It was one of the first churches in Pokhara and had grown out of the ministry of Green Pastures hospital. When we first arrived they were meeting in a tiny room made of rough concrete blocks and a tin roof. Over two hundred Nepalis sat cross-legged on the mud floor, men on the right and women and children on the left. When I say cross-legged, there wasn't actually enough room to let your thighs rest on the floor. Each knee was comfortably squashed onto your neighbours' knees. The overflow stood peering in from the windows and doorways. Some even clambered up the rails on the window to get a better view and to get a bit more comfortable.

I settled myself on the women's side, easing my sari to allow the greatest possible knee rest to occur. On almost every female lap there seemed to be either a suckling baby between the sari folds, or a toddler or two crawling happily over as many knees as possible. The women took it all in their stride. They even seemed to follow the songs and Bible talk as well as manage the children for the customary two- to three-hour service. I thought I had just run a marathon as I attempted to unfold my aching body back into an upright position after the service was over. I slowly manoeuvred my knees backwards and wondered whether I would ever completely straighten out again. Possibly not. But I quickly began to treasure those Saturday mornings in Nepali church.

In those early months my limited grasp of the language meant that I didn't catch much of the sermon. If I followed what the Bible passages were and caught a few key words then I thought I was doing well. But I fared better in the songs. We had learnt *dev nagari* script very early on, so I could theoretically read anything. All the Nepali songs were of course written in the *dev nagari* script, so as long as I could figure out the number and find it before the song finished, then I could sing along. A wonderful thing! It quickly made me feel part of Nepali worship. I would look around me at the upturned faces and join my voice with theirs for the next two hours. Of course, the more hours, the better. It didn't matter in the slightest that I usually had no idea what I was singing about, nor indeed what any of the words actually meant. I soon learnt that there was something of far greater importance than a perfect word-for-word translation and that was, of course, a thankful heart, a heart that wants to sing praises to God, anywhere and always because of his goodness, his mercy and his never-ending faithfulness.

5

A SEASON OF EXPECTATIONS
Pokhara, Nepal

Years later people asked me, 'What did you struggle with most in your day-to-day life in Nepal?' I'm not sure. There wasn't actually any one thing. But, on a bad day, all the little things could accumulate. I would bake bread every day, sifting through the hungry weevils to find the flour. As soon as the loaf had risen and was ready to go in the little box oven, the *bijuli* would go off. Then someone would be at the door. There was always someone at the door – wanting something: a visa to Australia, clothes, food, money, a bicycle. Sorting through the requests for genuineness sometimes seemed harder than sorting through the flour for weevils.

One particular beggar lady came often. She must have been about fifty. Her thin hair was tied up in a knot at the back. Her worn red sari had seen better days. She had very few teeth. She also had very little language that I could understand. I would usually give her a cup of *chammal* (uncooked rice), and she would go on her way. That was the extent of our interaction. One day she came and I had run out of *chammal*. There was nothing to give her. What would I do? The bread had just been baked. It was golden and light and smelled perfect so I cut her a slice and spread it with jam. It looked delicious. Well, this was just not acceptable to her. She virtually threw it in my face, she was so disgusted. And then she sat down on my doorstep and refused to move till I gave her something more enticing.

She had stamina. So did I. Four hours later she was still there. I had been busy inside writing letters and updating my leprosy research. And there was still no *chammal*. She became fed up. Before I knew it, she was around the back of the house, turning on our tap and letting the precious water run unhindered down the toilet. Well now I was fed up. I met her at the toilet and vented my annoyance on her, in very expressive English. Of course, she didn't understand a word, but she scampered off and I went back to my work. Half an hour later I thought I heard more commotion. Looking up again, there were now four fat buffalo in our back garden. She had apparently opened the gate and they'd wandered in and demolished our entire crop of *makai* (corn) in one fell swoop . . . months of labour and growth. I stared at the discarded stalks that lay trampled through the mud and struggled a great deal to stay calm. Arggghhh!

But quite apart from the little things, there was one thing that I regularly struggled with and that was the sense of living up to the expectations of our supporters back home in Australia. It was certainly not that they ever put us under any pressure to produce results. They were, by and large, a most wonderful group of praying, faithful, loving individuals. They believed that God had led us to Nepal and they wanted to support our work there. They gave generously of their time and money to allow us to live and work in Nepal. Twelve years on, as I write this, many of our original supporters are still giving, praying, writing to us, encouraging us, loving us from afar. We couldn't be here without them.

I think it was quite possibly because they were so beautiful that I felt an inner pressure to do something good. Even if the supporters had no expectations of us, I easily had them of myself. Whether from our church, our friends, the mission, myself, it was easy to move into a season of expectations; a season of wanting to do something good. If all those friends were sacrificially giving from what they had, then I needed to make good use of that giving. I felt that we needed to make good use of our time in Nepal. We needed to do the things that the Lord had planned for us to do and not waste time. Instead, we had to find those things and do them with our whole hearts. But what were those things that he had prepared in advance for us to do? Was it going to be that simple? Is it ever?

The questions

When we earned our own living back in Australia, it felt like we went for long periods without particularly questioning what we were doing or why. We were simply living: paying off the mortgage, doing a good job, buying food and other necessities for life. Along the way, opportunities to serve came our way and that was a bonus. But in our first three years in Nepal we were suddenly confronted by the bigger questions of life and purpose on a daily basis. We would air them on Friday nights with Andrew.

Darren constantly questioned whether he was making the best use of his time in the hospital. 'How is doing a purely clinical load going to be of any use to Nepal in the long run? It's just not sustainable.' He badly wanted to train Nepali physiotherapists, but in those years there was no accredited course and no potential trainees. He would come home after a long day and mull over the usefulness of his day. He had certainly benefited lots of individual patients and he was able to tell story after story of these but was there something better? Was there something more profitable? Was there something that would meet his expectations of himself? Surely there was.

Over time he began the long process of helping to develop an accredited national physiotherapy course. But that took another ten years (and another ten or so physios) to come about. As I write this, in 2005, we are reaping the benefits and happily teaching on that very course. But back in 1994, we couldn't see the end from the beginning. I guess that's the thing about seasons – we don't know what's coming next. We don't know that God doesn't waste a moment or an experience or a season. He has a plan from the beginning and he will carry it through to completion. But that's so much easier to see in hindsight.

I had similar quandaries with the way I spent my time at Green Pastures. I wanted to do the things that were the most helpful, especially those things that the Nepali physiotherapy technicians either weren't trained to do or weren't gifted to do. That worked out OK with the disability research and some dabbling in prosthetics with Sarah. It felt like it was 'something good', but the more confusing issue was that only one of us really needed to work in order to get a resident's visa. Did that mean I should be spending more of my time in other areas like the church and the community? I constantly asked myself these questions and struggled with the most important one: how could I best use my gifts to love Nepalis as he had loved me?

Fortunately for me, our Nepali pastor was a man of great vision and enthusiasm. He knew that we would be in Nepal for a time-limited season, so he was keen for us to find our niche in the church. He spent a long time one evening letting us talk through our gifts, or lack thereof, and helping us see where we could fit.

As a result, Darren soon found himself in the midst of twenty or so youth from our church. They would meet on a Friday night for what started off as another mini church service: the same songs, the same announcements, the same sermon and the same lack of involvement from the audience. The concept of interactive discussion hadn't really taken off in Nepal yet and that made sense given the rote learning method of education across the country. But discussion was what Darren craved and what God had gifted him for.

I've discovered that God doesn't generally hand out gifts and then give you nothing to do. He gives the opportunities as well as the gifts. It would probably be a waste of his time if he didn't. The opportunities can look different from season to season but, nevertheless, he still gives them. Half a dozen young Nepali men, including Shankar, seemed to keep appearing and they were keen to learn how to lead a Bible study. Darren was really keen to work with them and learn from them. They were also exceptional in their love for the Lord and they and their wives became our closest friends.

Not only was our pastor a man of vision and enthusiasm but he was also a most splendid evangelist. He was born a Hindu priest. When he was converted in the 1960s, his heart was for the unreached across the country. In a land of 20 million (mostly Hindus) spread across remote impassable terrain, this was some call. He trekked for days and weeks on foot to the most remote parts of Nepal telling of the saving grace of Jesus and the freedom found in him. Of the seventy-five districts in Nepal, he trekked through seventy-two of them. He would live wherever he could find a place to rest. If no house was welcoming, he would sleep in caves or under the stars, at the mercy of wild animals, the elements and hunger. He suffered numerous recurring bouts of malaria. It was during this time that he wrote what became one of the most popular Nepali hymns. It found its way into the Nepali hymn book as number 91. The translation doesn't do it justice, but verse three goes something like this:

> I can see the glory of heaven,
> Even though I didn't earn it.

I give you my deepest praise,
For this is all I have to give.
I put you on the throne of my heart.
Remain there on my heart.

Whenever I sing that song now, I picture Resham sleeping out under the stars, hungry and cold or sick with fever – yet seeing heaven. He faced opposition from the Hindu authorities on every journey. He was arrested, tortured and sent to jail three times. To this day his knee bears the scars of torture: it no longer bends as it should. He walks with a slight limp. But Resham's heart is all for the Lord. Even in jail, he shared from morning to evening about how the Lord had changed his life for good. He served a living God not a block of stone, he said, a God of love who had given him his life. Again the authorities weren't impressed. They came to assert their authority and to silence him but Resham remained calm. 'I preached the word of God out there, so you put me in here. Now I preach the word of God in jail. So where are you going to put me?' He was not bothered by their threats.

He would most often quote from 2 Corinthians 5:9: 'So we make it our goal to please him, whether we are at home in the body or away from it.' In fact, pleasing God was the main thing he did talk about, the main thing he thought about and the main thing he lived.

A correspondence course

In 1992, Resham and Sita, his wife, decided that they could reach many more people via the postal system, particularly given the state of the terrain, so they began a Bible correspondence course. Each course was a series of five booklets with questions at the end. Each booklet described the incredible love of God, found in

Jesus. If the students completed the five, they would receive a Bible. Resham and Sita started out with 100 names and addresses of people who were interested in the gospel. They operated out of boxes in their bedroom. Five years on, in 1997, the number exceeded 180,000 people. One hundred and eighty thousand people had requested the gospel and heard the good news and been changed as a result.

During that time, the operation outgrew the boxes in the bedroom. Resham and Sita followed up with discipleship training courses and leadership training courses. They sent out teams to help with church planting. Keen Nepalis went out two by two, travelling nine months of the year, through rain and snow, on foot, in order to reach the students. The students were now spread through every single one of the seventy-five districts, from the flat plains to the Tibetan border.

Thirteen years on, the door remains wide open. The course still runs and has reached more than 320,000 people. Letters pour in from all over the country describing lives changed and hearts touched by the love of God. 'We used to bow down to gods of stone. They were dead. They didn't speak to us and we were afraid of them. They never told us about love or about life. They didn't tell us about the Living God. But now we know him and he is the God we serve. He has made us new and given us peace. He has sent us his Son and now we want to live for him.'

My involvement in the Bible correspondence course was to help with any English translations they needed. Donors gave money to help with the publications, so newsletters in English were required. That was the easy bit. I would also sit in on committee meetings and attempt to follow the discussions and planning in Nepali. I remember one vividly. Letters had come in describing massive response across the country. Twenty thousand people were professing new faith. But the question became – how were they going to follow up that many people? Resham turned to me, 'How do you follow up new converts in your country?' I smiled to myself. My mind tried to reach back into my 'other life'. I couldn't remember a time back in Sydney when we ever discussed following up 20,000 people. If only we did have such dilemmas! What a privilege to live in a country where God is doing such a work. What a privilege to be part of it.

On another occasion, the police got wind of the activities of the Bible correspondence course. They walked up the three flights of stairs while we were sitting in the tiny office discussing the next journey of *The Jesus Film*. But one of our staff got there first and warned us. Without a moment to think, an INF colleague grabbed all the minutes and documents and we slipped around the corner and hid under the stairs.

For the next half-hour we hid there while the authorities again questioned Resham and Sita. They must have been given the words to say because nothing untoward eventuated. We were given the all-clear and another round of Nepali *chiya* before the meeting carried on as usual: how many new staff can we employ to answer letters and reach the furthest districts?

The smaller picture

Wherever there is a big picture at work, there is also a smaller picture. At times when the big picture becomes overwhelming it's good to be able to home in on the smaller picture. I caught a glimpse of that every Saturday at church. Many of the newer women who would sit near me seemed to be following the talk well but they couldn't read the Bible for themselves. They were illiterate, so they also couldn't find the numbers in their song books or even turn the pages in the right direction.

Finding chapter and verse in their Bibles was also impossible. That was OK if there was a family member at home who was happy to read it to them but often there wasn't and the women were hungry to read the Bible for themselves. Thankfully, there were some excellent literacy resources available in those days and it was relatively simple to set up groups of women and simply go through the books.

I remember the first day Lalu read her own name. She was 33. We were huddled near a candle in our front room because the *bijuli* was off again. She had spent the afternoon trying to make sense of the new *dev nagari* marks in her exercise book. But the afternoon had been long and they were still just marks . . . nothing more. It had been a grindingly slow process and I was feeling as tired as she was. Perhaps we'll call it a day, I thought. I was packing away the books when suddenly her face lit up. The candlelight danced in her eyes.

'It's my name! LA-LU!' She said, laughing until the bangles on her wrist almost came to life.

She knew who she was. She had a name and she could read it. The next week she read a road sign that she had passed every day of her life and never been able to read. But suddenly she was able to read it and even follow the directions. Gradually, she also began reading her Bible. She underlined everything in red because everything was marvellous to her. She never seemed to put it down and during that same time we became prayer partners. I now think that praying with Lalu was probably the best thing I did during those early years in Nepal. It was even more than something good.

The first time I met her we were walking together over a mountain. It was Saturday afternoon and about thirty of us from church had made the long trek to a remote spot in the gorge for a baptism. Six new church members had professed their faith in Jesus and been dunked in the fast-flowing stream. Then we sang and gave thanks to our God who changes lives; who brings us out of fear and hopelessness. It was as we were making our way back up the rocky gorge that I noticed Lalu's face. She seemed to radiate peace.

I introduced myself and laughingly figured out that she was actually the wife of Saroj, one of Darren's keen young Bible study members. I should have known that. We had spent so much time with Saroj lately but one of the funny things about sitting with the sexes segregated in church is that it takes you twice as long to figure out who belongs to whom. But once we had established who we were, I was drawn into her story. Her mother had leprosy. Her father was dead. She had been married off at a young age to a Hindu man who had treated her poorly – so poorly that he had run off with someone else as soon as she was pregnant with their daughter. In Nepal, unmarried mothers become the scum of society. They no longer fit into any social structure and are often left to the mercies of the streets. But Lalu's mother heard of Jesus through GP hospital and they both became believers. Our church opened their arms to them in a love that they had never known before.

Then Lalu had met and married Saroj. He was a good man with a heart for Jesus but he was about to go to India for two years of Bible college and Lalu was illiterate. She was so worried about how she would cope alone without him and without the Bible being read to her for two years. And that's why we began to meet together weekly to pray and read together. She never missed a session over the next two years, and became a faithful and true friend. I've been indescribably blessed by her friendship.

Being busy with 'good things' makes you feel better, particularly in a season where the perceived weight of other people's expectations feels too heavy. It certainly helped me to cope with the expectations that I felt were on us. It also makes writing newsletters easier. When you're involved in 'good things', there's always something interesting to write about, something that you feel will impress the audience or sounds fruitful and makes good use of their support money. And by and large they're very good things. Of course they are . . . serving in the hospital, researching leprosy, running literacy groups for women, helping out at the Bible correspondence course. They're good things and they're things that bear fruit for the Kingdom.

But our motives foil us at times. If my primary motive for being busy with good things is to please the supporters, then I may as well go home. At some point during that season, I remember reading this sentence from an unknown source: 'Learn to live for an audience of One'. So often, I was aware I was living for an audience of about 2,000. But I *wanted* to live for an audience of One. I wanted to do my living for him, my moments and my days, my comings and my goings. The desires of my heart were his but I was so easily distracted by the larger audience.

Perhaps our motives are never pure. Perhaps it's a lifelong battle to keep our eyes on him and to keep the other audience at bay. Maybe it is, but I think there are some seasons where the battle intensifies and the other audience looms louder than normal. Maybe it's helpful to notice when we're in a season like that and be aware of our responses.

It was during my prayer times with Lalu that I got the greatest sense of God just saying to me that he wanted me to 'be'; that being in him and remaining in him was far more important than the 'doing', even the doing of good things. 'Mission is all about going, not a lot about doing and everything about being' (unknown). The strange thing seems to be that the more we focus on 'being' and the less we focus on 'doing', the more we see God at work around us.

Burraburra

One more story, mostly about 'being', mostly about God. During one particular week, we had spent every night memorising John chapter one in our Nepali Bible. 'In the beginning was the Word, and the Word was with God, and the Word was God . . .' In Nepali it read: '*Aadima bochon hunnuhuntyo, bochon Paremaswarsung hunnuhuntyo, ani bochon Paremaswar . . .*' By the end of the week, we had it in our heads and we had figured out all the necessary vocabulary. I'm not quite sure why we chose John chapter one, but nevertheless we did and it seemed as good a place to start as any.

Feeling tired at the end of the week, we decided (along with Andrew) that we needed a weekend break. On a few other occasions we'd taken a short overnight trek to a village called Mirsa. It was lovely to be out in the hills, to wander through villages, watch whatever was being harvested in the fields and gaze upwards at the Himalayas. We had made friends with the headman in Mirsa and he happily welcomed us to sleep above the buffalo and share in his *dal bhat*, so we planned to take another trip there. And having been there a number of times before, we probably weren't concentrating on the directions so much. We were busy taking in the scenery and the goings-on around us. We watched children carrying large slabs of slate on their heads, mothers planting rice in the fields and fathers ploughing fields behind their buffalo.

By about 4 p.m. on the Saturday afternoon, it became obvious that we were nowhere near where we thought we were. In fact, we had very little idea of where we were at all. With dusk on the way we decided we should just stay at the next village we came to. It turned out to be a place called Burraburra. Mildly disappointed that we wouldn't be seeing our headman friend again, we went in search of a new headman.

This headman was also friendly and we were soon ensconced on the wooden slats of his balcony, overlooking the village. It was that time of the evening when the buffalo were being milked and the chickens were finding their place to roost. No sooner had we also settled into our roosting place, than along came two young lads from the family, hesitantly at first.

They began by saying they really wanted to practise their English with us. There's nothing very surprising in that. Almost every young Nepali is looking for an opportunity to practise their English. On a good day we happily oblige and it was a good day. Rather, it was a good evening. But it soon became clear that they had something specific on their minds. They didn't just want an ordinary English conversation. They wanted a specific English conversation because they had found a specific document in English and wanted it translated. So we encouraged them to bring it out and show us so we could see what it was all about.

The younger lad went off in search of it, came back and calmly handed us a small blue tract. We turned it over. It was John chapter one in English. 'Please tell us what it means,' he pleaded.

It was the only chapter of the Bible that we could explain in Nepali at that point in time. Out of the 1,189 chapters in the Bible they had found the only one we could easily chat about. They were desperate to understand it. We were in awe. If God cares about those two souls enough to take us to their village on a specific weekend, he cares about you too. He cares about every single one of us. That's enough for me.

6

A SEASON OF LONGING
Pokhara, Nepal

If meeting expectations was a struggle for me, close on its heels came a struggle of an entirely different nature. I longed for a child. I read somewhere that women can wake up one day and suddenly realise that their arms are empty. That certainly happened to me. It was April 1993 and we were still in India. I woke up that day to the sun already heating up the hospital compound. It was searing the dust between the pebbles. All signs of life had gone off in search of some early rains.

But I didn't notice the day. What I noticed was that my arms were empty. They even felt different. As I put the rice on to reheat, I looked down at them and, in particular, at the curve in my elbows. I tried to imagine filling up the curve with a warm bundle of milk-scented baby. I tried to imagine rocking the baby until it fell into a contented sleep. I tried to imagine the way it might snuggle in against me or the way I might gaze at its closed eyelids.

At some point during that bone-dry day in April my imaginings turned into longings and they were so deeply there that I couldn't believe I hadn't noticed them before. But I simply hadn't. They hadn't even existed. The day before, my arms hadn't been empty but now suddenly they were empty and that was how they remained for quite a while, or so it seemed during that season.

In most of our lives as women of the West, we can pretend that we have a reasonable amount of control over what comes our way. We order our home and our work environment. We plant out the garden (or the balcony as the case may be). We plan our weekends to catch up with friends and family, and we attempt to maintain healthy relationships and lifestyles. By all intents and purposes we are in control. We say yes to the things that are important to us and we say no to the things that aren't. Or we try to, on a good day.

For many of us, facing up to issues of reproduction is the first time that we face our complete inadequacy to order our world the way we would like it to be or the way that would follow our clever plan. We can spend hours and days working out the best month to conceive or the best year to begin our family and why that would fit so perfectly into our working schedule and the other commitments that we have.

At best it's a pretence. Every now and again you do hear stories of women for whom it all worked out 'perfectly'. I actually think that they're the exception . . . they're merely the most vocal. After hundreds of conversations with women, I've hardly spoken with anyone who actually conceived each child when they planned to or who didn't lose pregnancies along the way or who didn't shed tears at some point during their reproductive life.

I certainly shed tears. In the beginning it was merely the monthly disappointment, which became worse each time. I became acutely attuned to the symptoms of PMT, which were always on their way. The progesterone kick brought more than its usual tenderness and irritability. It brought 'failure' every time and the fear of 'Will it ever happen?' It brought misery.

On the other hand, of course, was my desire to trust God for whatever he had in mind for us. It's such a hard place to be, month in and month out. I knew that our times were in his hands and that his plans were far beyond mine, but it's all very well to know great amounts of truth in your head. Transferring that truth to the heart level is another matter altogether. At a heart level, the pain still sits and then guilt creeps in quietly. Why can't I just trust him for his purposes?

As I write this, I am aware of many of my friends whose struggle to have children was much greater than mine. Their agony was prolonged and, for some, the issues remain unresolved today. Their agony continues. But I write this chapter because I think there's a season called 'longing'. It touches all of us, at one time or another, in various ways and circumstances. It doesn't matter what country we're in or what vocation we're following, 'longing' may emerge, often as an unexpected season and one that we didn't count on or weren't prepared for. I certainly wasn't.

Being in Nepal certainly made it trickier. Wherever you are when you decide to start a family and find it's not that simple, you'll almost certainly be surrounded by pregnant friends and relations and complete strangers. They jump out at you in the bazaar, or stand up behind you on the bus, and then they start a random conversation – just when you thought you were kind of doing OK today. There they are waiting for you – a trigger to remind you of what you don't have and to kick the issue back into a higher level of consciousness. We, of course, were inundated with letters from Australia announcing pregnancies and, sometime later, childbirth. Photos and stories full of joy were sent our way.

But it wasn't just the folks back in Australia. Even amongst the *bideshi* community in Pokhara in those days, we were the only young couple without children. It seemed at least half of the INFers were either pregnant or caring for babies. It certainly has its challenges (as well as joys) being part of a small community. I think it's possible to lose that sense of 'normal' that you can foster back in a big city like Sydney where there's always someone who's exactly at your life stage and eager to spend time with you. In Nepal there was no such choice. But God still provides. Linda had become a dear friend and prayer partner, and if it hadn't been for her love and encouragement I may not have survived that season.

My childlessness was highlighted in ways that it wouldn't have been in a wider community. But it wasn't just the human population. Even the animal kingdom served to point out my lack. Everywhere I walked there were fluffy ducklings trailing after their mother. There were piglets snuffling around in the mud and baby goats gambolling. There were signs of fertility everywhere. It sounds pathetic, I know. But perhaps, at a basic level, that's what we are. We live here in this world and we don't actually get everything we want, when we want it. We wait and wait and then we wait some more. During the waiting, we see-saw between acceptance and joy and then we immediately plummet back into deep sadness, never knowing what tomorrow will bring. And that is, of course, the worst bit. If we knew how long the waiting would be, the season wouldn't really be a season of longing.

The other difficulty in Nepal was that we didn't really have access to the anonymous medical help that you crave at a time like that. And yes, it was pre-Internet. So after it had all been going on for well over a year, I happened upon a fairly comprehensive medical text. It stated, to my horror, that, 'Infertility is defined by the inability to conceive after a year of trying.' I was officially infertile! Quite shocked, I started to wonder whether we should seek help, or at least a test or two. But from where? The questions sat uncomfortably.

In the meantime, I dwelt more on the waiting. Perhaps I need to learn to wait in order to grow, I thought. Maybe if I never waited for anything, I'd never grow. Maybe if I never hoped for things unseen, I'd never learn. And if I can't hope for things unseen on this earth, then how will I hope for things unseen in the world to come? And if I had already seen these things, where would be my faith? Where would be my dependence on God? Where would be my ability to cry, 'How great Thou art!'?

I think there's something altogether different about crying, 'How great Thou art!' from a heart that is longing for something unseen. Because at a deep level, I knew that regardless of his plan for me, I would cry, 'How great Thou art!' for the rest of my life. Regardless of whether God said yes or no to a child, I would still praise him – because he would still be God and he would still have my life in his hands. And if that meant rethinking the next twenty years then so be it. That's what I thought.

By June 1994 we were investigating adoption. Other INFers had successfully adopted Nepali orphans. They shared with us some amazing stories of God's plan and provision for them and the children. We began to feel quite inspired so we started the ball rolling with the Australian government and overseas adoption.

Then, on 27 June, we were sitting in an INF prayer meeting. These happened monthly on a Wednesday morning and were always a privilege to attend and be a part of. There's nothing quite like being in a room packed full of INFers, praying their hearts out for the nation and for its people that they love. They were of one mind and one vision: to bring the love of God through any means to the people of Nepal. They would move effortlessly in and out of prayer and praise songs for hours. This particular morning was much like every other except that Darren was convinced that he heard God speak to him. He felt that God said to him, 'You will have a son this time next year and he will be a man of prayer. He will pray for Nepal.'

When Darren related this to me later, I didn't know what to think. I was weary of the cycle of hope and disappointment. I knew that it was possible that Darren was just 'hearing' what he wanted to hear. We had been immersing ourselves in the stories of the Old Testament. Darren could easily have been subconsciously projecting a similar word onto us as in the days of Abraham and Isaac. And anyway, the Old Testament was all about the line of descent to Jesus – that was the point of it all. And I know that God still speaks today, through his word and his Spirit, but I also know that he doesn't *always* speak in the way that we want him to. He is God after all.

One sleepless night, I went and sat on our flat concrete roof. It was a full moon. In fact it seemed to be shining right down on my head. The stars were bright and reflecting off the Himalayas. And I was so sad. I poured my heart out to God again and the tears came freely. Time passed and I just sat there and very slowly the tears changed to peace, a new peace: whatever happens, I thought, I'm right with God. Whatever happens, I know I'm his. That's all I need to know. So I will wait.

7

A SEASON OF LIFE
Pokhara, Nepal

On 27 June 1995 we gave birth to our first child . . . a son. Exactly one year to the day since Darren felt that God spoke to him. The exact day.

The timing astounded us. You can't orchestrate these things. God spoke to Darren in the June of 1994 and then gave us a son exactly a year later. If the labour hadn't taken fifty-three hours it wouldn't have been that day. Sometimes it feels like God gives us an extra hug, an extra reminder of his presence. 'I'm in charge,' he says. 'I love you. I have plans for you and your children. I love him more than you do. I created him for a purpose and I will fulfil that purpose.'

His arrival was in true Nepali style. Years later, I would sit in Australia at my friends' baby showers and, inevitably, someone would start reliving a delivery story. The attention would shift to me, 'Go on, tell us what it was like giving birth in Nepal.' A few times I actually did try to tell the story but I knew it wasn't going to work. The story was nowhere near the world that they knew. It was certainly nowhere near the world of plush delivery suites and hot water baths. But it was very near to the hand of God.

During the month of June, we borrowed a friend's old motor scooter. It was small and blue and had a fairly annoying habit of completely stopping whenever it rained. It was something to do with the leads not liking getting wet. But it was great to be able to get around Pokhara more easily. Not that being nine months pregnant and zipping around on the back of a motor scooter was the most comfortable thing I've ever done. I started to think more about Mary and her long trip to Bethlehem on the donkey. If she had ridden side-saddle, I thought, I could definitely understand why . . . quite apart from the cultural and clothing issues. I copied.

On the night of 24 June, we took the motor scooter to a hotel in the tourist area of town to watch the Rugby World Cup final. I remember the red chairs and making myself comfortable. I vaguely remember a chicken dish. I remember nothing of the World Cup final. I have no idea who was even playing, let alone who won. I do remember starting to feel a bit weird, though, so I told Darren. He was fairly casual: 'We may as well watch the end of the game.'

So we did. At 10 p.m. we began the slow journey home on the motor scooter. It took us right around the lake, across the fields and down towards the bridge. Just before we hit the bridge it started to rain. Actually, in Nepal it rains every day in June, July, August and September. It was nothing very surprising, so we took it in our stride. After all, it was our third monsoon. For some reason we didn't have wet weather gear on.

Then the motor scooter puffed and hissed and gave up. There we were in the pitch black, in drenching rain, pushing the motor scooter home and that was when I felt my first real contractions. It was quite unmistakable. We were a good half-hour's walk from home. For some reason, the first thing that came into my head was what a good newsletter story it would make: 'Overseas worker gives birth in drenching rain under a bridge in Nepal.' I think I amused myself for the rest of the walk home, making up the rest of the story. 'The buffalo kept watch and the frogs joined in the chorus as the cries rent the air . . .' But it was only a story. We did actually get home, dry and sort of comfortable, in time to see what would happen next.

The first few hours of contractions in a first labour are just dreadfully exciting. After nine months of waiting, I was longing to see the baby's face, to feel skin on my skin, to begin the journey of mothering. In my naivety, I thought it would be any minute now. So Darren went running off, in the rain, to the house of the English midwife, who lived a twenty-minute walk away. She then showed up on her motor scooter which was the same model as ours except that, fortunately, it worked in the rain.

Wendy stripped off her more than adequate wet weather gear and took a good look at the mother-to-be. The bad news was that I was only one centimetre dilated. I was so disappointed. Part of me didn't even believe it. The contractions had been coming five minutes apart, but I guess they weren't that regular. And they certainly weren't agony yet. But I wasn't to know what was coming. Nevertheless, Wendy thought it might be sensible to move me up to the hospital (WRH) anyway. It was the middle of the night but they called for the INF vehicle from GP and off I went in style. Well, style compared to the motor scooter.

And that was the beginning of my introduction to the WRH maternity ward. I found my way to a two-bedded ward. On the other bed was a young Nepali girl, in an advanced stage of labour. Surrounding her were at least twenty of her relatives. They sat on the bed with her, they crouched on the floor, they took up every inch of the room. They coughed and spluttered, they rambled on in Nepali and they stared at me. In my befuddled state, I stared back.

I vaguely wondered how I would get my pregnant belly from the doorway to the other bed. The other bed was of course the furthest one from the door and between it and me were all the bodies. The more I stared at them, the more I noticed that the bodies weren't moving. So that could only mean one thing: I had to do the moving. But there was a problem. Clambering over bodies in the middle of labour wasn't easy. It hadn't featured in the childbirth manuals I'd read. But then again, restarting your clapped-out motor scooter in the middle of labour hadn't featured either.

For the rest of that night, then a whole day, then another night, the contractions kept coming and I was exhausted. About every ten minutes I needed to visit the toilet again. The toilet, of course, was a long way away. I would somehow clamber over all the relatives again (perhaps I should write my own manual) and limp down the corridor, contracting away, to find the squat toilets ever overflowing with unmentionable contents and in dire need of a gallon of water. Even to empty them by a fiercely long pole into the physio room would be better than this!

At some point in my now hazy memory, I think the girl and her entourage must have gone away. But in their place came a whole new set of onlookers. Because Darren worked at the hospital, the entire staff knew him and the word got around quickly: 'The young *bideshi* girl is in labour. She keeps moaning. You should go and have a look. It's really interesting . . .'

And look they did. At first they came in dribs and drabs. Three nurses from the orthopaedic ward, two pharmacists from downstairs, a nursing assistant from the burns ward. They came in and just stared. Some of them sat down on the bed to have a nice little chat in Nepali with me. How to cope with visitors wanting polite little chats in Nepali is another thing that isn't generally covered in childbirth manuals. Eventually, even Darren got fed up with it. The door was barred. We only let the midwife in.

About forty hours after arriving in the hospital, I was still getting nowhere. During a lull in the contractions, Darren went off to kick-start our prayer chain in Australia. The situation probably warranted it. We were in big trouble. It was even beginning to look worse than our first bout of diarrhoea in India.

Then Wendy had a brainwave. She must have decided that the maternity ward toilet and onlooker situation wasn't really conducive to a relaxed childbirth experience. So she broke INF protocol and said that we could go to her place and have the baby there. We somehow walked the five minutes around the corner and found her little stone house in the lane behind the hospital.

What a relief! There was a Western toilet. There's nothing quite so lovely in the middle of labour as a Western toilet. The thing is, you can actually rest on it. And it was clean. As well as that, she had a proper cane chair to sit on, with two cushions. They were very pretty cushions with blue and red flowers. I eased myself down, I leant back and I gazed around me. For the first time in days, I took a deep breath in.

A time to love . . .

In another contraction-free moment I found my Bible. I'm not in the habit of just opening it at random. But I did that day. There was no time for a systematic context study. It opened at Psalm 108:6:

> Save us and help us with your right hand, that those you love might be delivered.

Now, I really do know that the psalmist was talking about a different kind of deliverance. But on that day, after forty-four hours of labour in the hills of Nepal, the Lord spoke to me: 'The baby is one that I love. I will deliver him.' And he did (with a little bit of help from Wendy). Finally, early on Tuesday morning, Stephen arrived, head first, weighing in at 1.9kg. He was tiny and blonde and gorgeous. I fell in love.

Our less polite friends said that he looked like a skinned rabbit. I never saw it myself. But I must admit, he wasn't a dimply baby. He fitted in the palm of Darren's hand. He was altogether tiny. His tiny little nose perched perfectly above his tiny little mouth, which sat above the tiny little indent in his chin . . . I breathed it all in. I didn't take my eyes off him.

I carefully wrapped him up in the blue bunny rug that had been sent from Australia. I noticed that, wrapped up in the rug, he fitted perfectly in the empty curve in my elbow. I held and he snuggled. It was delightful. He was perfect in every way, but there was a problem. He was too tiny to suck. In hindsight, a Western hospital would have whisked him away to a neonatal intensive care unit. He would have been nicely fitted out with every conceivable tube attached to his body. There was no such thing in Pokhara. There was not even a trace of a humidicrib.

So we did the only thing we could do. We nursed him day and night. I expressed milk onto a perfectly sterile teaspoon and dribbled it into his mouth, every hour, all through the day and all through the night. It was not just *on* the hour, it was all through the hour. Getting enough dribbling nourishment into him was more than a full-time job, it was my life. For the whole first month I expressed and dribbled and cuddled. I must have gone into survival mode. I certainly don't remember sleeping.

One day during that first month, we had to take Stephen to the Australian Embassy in Kathmandu for his citizenship papers. That meant a ten-hour Nepali bus trip. How was I going to do my hourly expressing? I don't think my Nepali fellow travellers would have taken kindly to it. Besides that, the bumpy roads and terrifying bends would have been a challenge. For that day only, he somehow managed to suck. I have no idea how.

Darren and Naomi,
1984

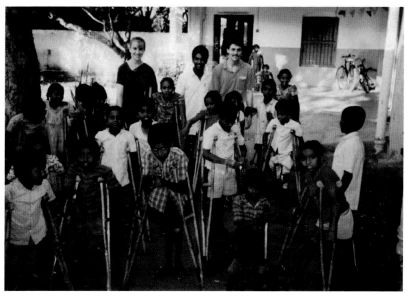

St Mary's Polio Home, Khammam,
South India

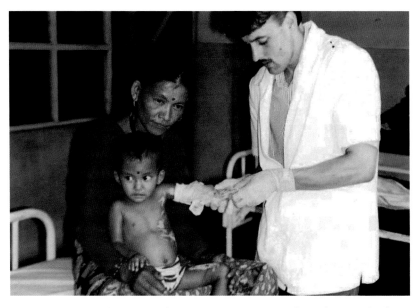

Darren treating a patient at Western Regional Hospital,
Pokhara, Nepal

A patient at Green Pastures Leprosy
Hospital, Pokhara

The little yellow house,
Pokhara

Darren and Naomi near their home
in Pokhara

Lalu with two-day-old
Stephen

Collecting water in
a doko

Darren, Naomi and Stephen enjoying
the crowd

Naomi and Jeremy, the main bazaar,
Pokhara

With Lalu's family,
2003

In Dhulikhel bazaar,
2004

Disappearing into the paddy,
Dhulikhel, Nepal

Sunday school in
Dhulikhel

Heading down the hill,
Dhulikhel

Nepali women carrying firewood and
water in the rain

There are some seasons when it seems like the mundane takes over. For reasons outside our control, we are suddenly flung into a lifestyle pattern which is made up of details. We simply have to get through the details. In order to survive, we burrow down and get on with it. It takes up all our reserves of strength and energy until it feels like there's nothing left over. Indeed, there probably is nothing left over.

But I think that's actually OK during those seasons. What else can we do? Spiritually, it can seem like an 'off season'. I was no longer praying with the urgency with which I'd prayed during my season of longing. I was hardly praying at all (except for more grace during the long and exhausting nights). I was no longer yearning for heaven as I had during my season of enrichment. Instead, I was fully taken up with the 'now'. It seemed like the image of heaven had all but disappeared.

But I have to say here that I really do think God understands. He knows that we are buried under the details. He knows that we have moved into survival mode. He also knows better than we do that the season will pass. We will lift our heads up again and see the sky once more. We will see trees waving in the wind. We will remember. We will remember the God who made us, who delights in us and who was just as present during that season as any other. And we will give thanks.

Parenting in Nepal

Two days after Stephen's birth, we somehow made it back to our little yellow home down the lane. We stepped out of the taxi and were mobbed. Every Nepali in the neighbourhood had come for a look at the tiny white baby.

'What's his name?' they all asked.

'*Singh Bahadur*,' replied Darren, laughing. They all smiled.

They looked down again at our tiny bundle with the bald head and the white face. *Singh Bahadur* means 'Brave Lion' in Nepali. The name, of course, stuck.

There are all sorts of 'must-dos' after you give birth in Nepal. I found them out one by one . . . purely because I managed to do every single one of them wrong. The first thing you should do is stay inside the house for one month. I found that out as soon as I left the house to go to church on the first weekend. The neighbours again crowded around and wanted to know where we were going and why.

'But you must stay in the house! You mustn't go out!'

The next infraction came immediately afterwards. 'But you are not wearing a *patuka*!' This, seemingly, was even worse. A *patuka* is a very long and wide piece of material that should be wrapped about twenty times around your waist and then worn constantly for the first three months after childbirth. 'If you don't wear a *patuka* you will have a sore back and you will stay fat,' they said. Actually, as I write this, three babies later, I think that *patukas* have their advantages . . . but at the time I wasn't overly keen. Mainly because it was so hot.

And apparently, it wasn't just me who should have stayed wrapped. In the middle of July in 30-degree heat in Nepal, babies must *always* have a *topi* (woolly hat) on. The neighbours were so upset about it that I would carry one up my sleeve. Whenever I saw a concerned neighbour approaching, I would whip it out and deftly cover Stephen's head before the recriminations began. I got very good, and very fast, at it.

Then, there are all sorts of complicated rules about food. Every food item is divided into 'hot' and 'cold' categories which seems to have nothing to do with whether the food is actually hot or cold in a temperature sense or even in a spicy sense. To this day I still haven't figured out the definitions. But there was definitely appropriate food and very inappropriate food, and whenever a Nepali friend dropped in they would catch me eating very inappropriate food. Bread and jam, spaghetti and yoghurt, peanut butter, bananas . . . Then, of course, they would notice that the baby had some wind.

'See! Of course he has wind! You're eating all the wrong foods!'

It was easier to figure out the appropriate food. My Nepali friends came to visit us loaded down with gifts of appropriate food: packets of savoury biscuits, three dozen mangos and four chickens. Then the same again the next day . . . and the next day. It went on like that for the whole first month. I was overwhelmed by their generosity. These were friends who only had one small light bulb in the house because they couldn't afford the electricity bill. Yet they spent their last rupee on chicken for me.

Years later, friends in Australia would question me: 'Didn't you think of coming home to have the baby?'

I raised one eyebrow just the tiniest bit. 'But I was at home.'

They were right in lots of ways. It certainly would have been easier to have the baby in Australia. There would have been clean surfaces, hot running water, mothercraft nurses, disposable nappies and neonatal units.

But I wouldn't have known the love of my Nepali friends. I think it seemed to them that the tables were turned. Finally they could help me. Finally they could love me. I was in their place, doing what they do: having babies.

Quite close to our house was a little lane filled with very poor shack-type houses. The women were always out the front washing clothes and picking nits out of each other's hair. I would walk past them most days on my way to the bazaar. I longed to speak to them, but I felt like an outsider. Largely, they ignored me. This carried on for eighteen months. Then I had the baby. Suddenly I was no longer an outsider or a weirdo *bideshi*. I was one of them: a woman. We began to speak every day. It was nothing too deep, but it was a connection. I had been accepted; still strange, but accepted.

Another very positive aspect of having a baby in Nepal is that they can go wherever you go. I would wrap my *kasto* (shawl) around Stephen, then twice around my middle and off we would go. Whether it was the women's literacy group, the leprosy hospital, the language lesson, we were always together. We were always one. We were always talking and playing, wrapped up in our *kasto*.

Of course, crawling is another stage altogether. That's when I realised that mud floors and nice little outfits don't go together. Mind you, even concrete floors in the monsoon become grey floors. And nice little outfits become grey little outfits. I'm not quite sure why we bothered with colours.

When Stephen was 9 months old, we trekked up to the Langtang mountain range, some days north of Kathmandu. Andrew and Sara came too. If we thought we received attention in Pokhara, it was nothing compared to walking through villages at 10,000 feet with a white baby. The word would 'telegraph' on ahead. So by the time we reached the next *chiya* stop, the crowd was already gathered in anticipation. Friendly Tibetan women would claim him as their own, happily carrying him off to show all their friends and relations. Fortunately, Stephen was that sort of very obliging baby who smiled at every strange face that leered down at him. Thousands of them did.

Water problems

When we moved into the little yellow house, we were warned about the water problems. 'It's really bad,' they said. 'You won't cope. It's particularly bad in the monsoon: all the pipes get blocked and there's just nothing coming. You should look for another house.'

But of course we had just come from India and there was nothing we couldn't cope with, or so we thought. In hindsight, they were right about the water problems. We didn't particularly notice it when it was just the two of us. The pipes that led to the little tank on the roof did get blocked all the time, but we had an alternative. We would collect rainwater out the back in our black barrels and bucket it inside. We got the 'showering' thing down pat as well. We would allow each other two lots of 500 millilitres for the 'shower': one before the lather and one after. We were doing just fine.

Then along came cloth nappies. I never realised how much water it takes to wash eight cloth nappies a day. I began to understand why Nepalis don't use nappies. In many ways the 'catch-it-as-he-goes' method is a lot easier . . . perhaps messier, but definitely easier and less costly on the water resources.

I remember one week in particular. It hadn't rained for a fortnight so we had used up all the water in the black barrels. Then the pipes to the roof tank blocked. Darren had chosen that week to go to Beni, a small town four hours' walk away, to conduct a physiotherapy camp. So there I was, on my own (with Stephen), watching the water vanish and watching the pile of very dirty and smelly nappies pile up. With each day the situation worsened and I was in a dilemma over what to do. I couldn't carry water from the nearest tap. It was a block away and I was still reeling from my attempts in India, realising that this time I had a baby to carry as well as the water jug (and no prams). I was definitely not keen.

By Thursday night, I realised that I only had one litre of water left for drinking purposes. I went to my room and prayed, 'Lord, I don't know what to do. Please send me some water.'

He did. Overnight the pipes unblocked and our tank filled to the brim. I awoke in the morning to the sound of it overflowing onto the roof . . . what a beautiful sound. He provides all that we need, and then some more.

Decisions

And so it was that in September 1996 our three-year term in Nepal came to an end. In the beginning, the season had seemed like it was stretching out into infinity. How could we cope for that long? Would we be remembered back in Australia? Would we thrive in this situation? Was it too long? What about our families back home?

The answers came slowly. We had made Nepal our home and it seemed to be a good fit for us. Language was getting easier and our friendships with Nepalis were developing. We were learning and being moulded in our walk with God. And we wanted to keep being available. So we started praying about the possibilities of returning to Nepal for a second three-year term. As we prayed, we thought we were open to what-ever he wanted for our lives – but would he make it clear this time?

At the same time, INF was making plans to open up a new centre in a town called Nepalgunj. Down on the flat border with India, this was a tough place to work. It was very hot in summer, covered in dust and dirt, and plagued with malaria. The hospital was a desolate place and had no physiotherapy input whatsoever. We went on a fact-finding mission and felt compelled to offer ourselves as potential members of the new team.

Although we felt compelled, it was a hard call. After our visit there, we could plainly see it would be difficult. There were no fancy hotels in which to watch the World Cup final. There were no restaurants for anniversary outings. There were no other families in the new team. I worried about whether I would cope without other young mothers who I could go to for advice. One day, I was sitting in prayer. Actually I was sitting in worry more than anything. Then a verse from Isaiah 58 came to me:

> The LORD will guide you always; he will satisfy your needs in a sun-scorched land and will strengthen your frame. You will be like a well-watered garden, like a spring whose waters never fail.

When we earnestly seek after God, he does lead us. He shows us the path. And being on his path is so much more important than being somewhere 'comfortable' because when it's his path, he *satisfies* us. I needed to trust that he would make me a well-watered garden in the place of his calling, wherever that was, because it's not the environment that does the watering, it's the Lord himself. In fact, being a well-watered garden has nothing to do with the place where we are; it has only to do with who he is. I needed to be ready to go . . . so we said yes.

Then we packed up our dear little house in Pokhara, the house where we had brought up our first baby. He had learned to crawl on the roof and he had learned to walk in the garden. He had laughed at the pigs next door and gone for rides on the buffalo. There were so many special memories in that house and so many friends nearby. And here we were, heading off into the unknown again.

We put all our belongings in the damp and dusty INF shed. They would be ready to transport to Nepalgunj when we returned from home leave in six months' time. We said some quick goodbyes to our friends in Pokhara and boarded the plane . . . for the UK! We had this marvellous plan to be at Sara and Andrew's wedding on our way to Australia. But even as we were getting on the plane, we were firmly assuring our Nepali friends that we would see them again in no time at all.

We didn't know then about the seasons.

8

A SEASON OF GRIEF
Sydney, Australia

A time to speak . . .

The purpose of home leave is threefold. We were meant to catch up with our friends and family, have some relaxation time and update our supporters on the work in Nepal. We loved it. There's nothing quite as exciting as speaking publicly about God's grace and his plans and the way he draws people into a relationship with him. We counted up eighty-three meetings in those six months and covered five of Australia's states and territories.

Wherever we went, there seemed to be a flood of young people who were interested in overseas missions and were hungry to hear of opportunities to serve or to pray. They took us into their hearts and into their prayer lives. At a Bible college in Sydney so many people gathered around us to pray and lay hands on us, that we almost collapsed under the weight of it. One stranger who we had met at a speaking engagement rang us up every week to get more prayer points. He really wanted to pray more effectively for the work in Nepal. Everyone was keen to know about our plans and we readily told them our return dates the following year. The pledges towards our support costs were overflowing.

We were also just enjoying being in Australia. We took off our shoes whenever we could to remember the feel of carpet.

Stephen discovered baths . . . and bubble bath and swings and slippery dips. I feasted my eyes on gardens full of pretty flowers. We ate fancy cheeses and Weet-Bix and masses of chocolate. Darren bought a road bike and indulged himself on Sydney's bike paths. I wore shorts. And we all went to the beach as much as we could. There seemed to be an abundance of fine food, friends and family surrounding us all the time. We were feeling blessed.

Best of all, on Christmas Day we discovered that I was pregnant with our second child. We were overwhelmed with God's goodness and his impeccable timing. The baby was due in August and INF quickly agreed that we should extend our home leave, have the baby in Australia and then return to Nepalgunj, as planned. They had also been concerned about Stephen's low birth weight the year before and they affirmed our decision to have this baby where we would have access to good medical care.

Then we were given permission to stay on at the short-term flat in Westmead, Sydney. That was perfect because the flat was right next to the excellent teaching hospital where we had both previously worked – which actually made me look forward to childbirth! Darren found some part-time work for a few months. We even found our old car which our friends had been minding for us. Then, we heard that our INF friends in Nepal (also Australians) were expecting their second baby in the same week as ours. They would come home for the birth and we could all travel back to Nepal together. It couldn't have been better.

A tree planted by the water

At many of the meetings we attended in the first three months of 1997 we shared a verse from Jeremiah 17:7–8:

> Blessed is the man who trusts in the LORD, whose confidence is
> in him. He will be like a tree planted by the water that sends

out its roots by the stream. It does not fear when heat comes; its leaves are always green. It has no worries in a year of drought and never fails to bear fruit.

I'm not quite sure why we kept sharing from it. It just seemed to fit. We were particularly struck by it at the beginning of that year, especially the message that none of us knows what the year ahead holds. For some of us, it may indeed be a year of drought or a year of trials, we said. We don't know what's ahead. All that we can do is trust in him and plant ourselves deeply in his word and in his love for us. Then, whatever happens, our confidence is in him . . . because that's the only way that our leaves will stay green and our lives will stay fruitful.

We didn't know it then, but the message was for us.

In late March we found ourselves at a cross-cultural retreat for a whole week. Feeling very refreshed, we took the Friday off so that we could go and have our routine 18-week ultrasound of the baby. My folks had been staying with us and looking after Stephen for the week, so we trotted off happily, looking forward to seeing the baby up close and getting to know him or her.

I'll never forget the look on the doctor's face that day. He turned slowly around from the screen and just looked at us. 'I'm afraid I have some very bad news for you,' he said. 'The baby has died.'

Silence.

The cicadas stopped humming. The cleaners stopped cleaning. The beepers stopped beeping. There was only us, in a world that had stopped living.

He went on to explain the cause of death. 'The baby had anencephaly, a kind of spina bifida of the brain. It wasn't compatible with life.'

I remained silent, gripping Darren's hand. I don't even remember him saying anything. We just kept holding on to each other. In some other fuzzy land the doctor was asking us if we had any questions. Not getting any response, he left us alone for a while. We still didn't say anything. There was nothing to say.

The yellow walls of the cubicle began to swim around me. I noticed details like the washbasin and the wastepaper basket. A tray of needles lay untouched by the sink. Any minute now, the bed we were sitting on would float away.

The hospital staff came and went, wanting to know what decisions we would make. We wanted to go home. If we could just make it back to the flat, we might be able to go back to yesterday. I put my hand on my stomach. It was still there. I could feel it.

The staff came again. We had to make a choice: give birth to the dead baby or attempt an operation. I couldn't make the choice. I wanted yesterday.

We opted for a normal delivery and I was given some labour-inducing drugs but they didn't work. I was given some more. The night wore on. We were getting nowhere, except sadder and sadder. The bed was starting to float. By the morning, I knew we would have to have an operation. That would mean I would never see the baby's face. I would never hold it. But in some ways it was the easy option. It would draw a line on the agony.

I remember going under anaesthetic. The doctor was inserting the cannula into my wrist and I couldn't stop crying. At that exact moment some words of a song came into my mind: 'Strength for today, hope for tomorrow.' No other words came. There must be other words to that song but they didn't come – just those six words over and over again. That's what he gives. The Lord gives strength for today and hope for tomorrow. On that hospital bed, as I went under the anaesthetic, he reminded me that he would get me through that day and, when it was over, I would still be alive. And I would still be his – and he would give me hope for tomorrow.

The day did finally come to a close and I was aware of feeling empty. I was empty. There was nothing within me. For days I dreamt that the baby was still there but then I would wake up and it wouldn't be there. There was nothing within me.

A time to weep . . .

I was particularly teary during that first day in hospital. So much so that one of the nurses called for the social worker to come and see me. She made her way into the room, sat down on the chair and asked me why I was still crying.

I couldn't find any words. She seemed to think that my sadness was out of proportion to what I'd been through. Perhaps it was. But I was simply too sad to try to explain it to her. Perhaps if I could have stopped crying, I might have told her about our home in Nepal, our Nepali friends who were waiting for us to come home, the temporary nature of our time in Sydney, and then, our hopes and dreams for our child.

We had spent the last three months talking about the baby and how it would fit into our family. We had been overawed by God's perfect timing. Every detail had been in place for us to stay in Australia and then return to Nepalgunj after the baby was born.

In lots of ways, losing the baby meant more than losing our child. It meant that the hinge point of our lives was no longer there. It was a bit like we were throwing darts onto a dartboard but both the board and the wall had been taken away. Where did that leave the darts? Where did that leave the reasons we were staying in Australia, the flat we were living in near the hospital and Darren's part-time work arrangement? If the baby was no longer coming where did that leave us? What

country should we be in? We were too numb initially to talk
these matters through but they were sitting there between us,
edging their way out.

The seasons merge

Autumn came. I've never known an autumn quite like it. The
reds and golds of the liquid ambers were a sight for my sore
eyes. I couldn't stop staring at them. I felt the leaves crunch
beneath my feet and I let my eyes linger on the colours.
Perhaps it was because we hadn't had an autumn for five
years. Autumn is one season that Nepal and India just don't
'do', so its beauty overwhelmed me. But at the same time, I
wondered . . . was it possible to enjoy such beauty while feeling such grief? Could the two co-exist? How could beauty
carry on?

The answer is that they do. Even in pain, the joys of life still
bring a smile. The seasons do merge. They overlap. Beauty
creeps in while your back is turned. You're busy thinking that
grief is all there is, then suddenly something beautiful takes
you by surprise and you realise that you can still smile; that
smiling doesn't take away from the sadness.

Stephen was still a delight. I rejoiced in him more than ever.
Many people said, 'Be thankful that you still have Stephen,' or,
'At least you have one child.' At times, to be honest, I found
their comments insensitive. But they were right. I was very
thankful for Stephen. I would get up three times during the
night just to check on him, to take in his beloved 2-year-old
face. I would spend more time simply being with him, listening to his 2-year-old thoughts and understanding his 2-year-
old ways. Other friends would describe their agonies over the
'terrible twos'. I never saw it. Instead, I wondered whether I
would know the joy of a 2-year-old again.

We received so many heartfelt words of comfort during that time. The postman must have grown tired of us. The cards piled up and covered every inch of the flat and phrases from them passed through my mind as I moved through my day. I thought about joy and sorrow and I thought about comfort and loss. Very often, they come together.

The reason I was so sad was because I'd known joy. I was weeping for that which had been my delight. I came to realise, ever so slowly, that I was thankful that I'd known our child. I'd rather have carried the baby and lost it than never have carried it at all. Never to have known it or have had those special months together would have been unthinkable. I gradually moved towards thankfulness. Our pastor and a dear INF friend came over to help us grieve. We named the baby Maili (which means 'our second child' in Nepali) and we sang and read Scripture together. We seemed slowly to be able to move on.

9

A SEASON OF CONFUSION
Sydney, Australia

The immediate future loomed in our faces. We re-booked our aeroplane tickets to return to Nepal in May. It seemed clear. If we were not having another baby then we should return to Nepal because that was where our home and our work was. Staying at the short-term flats in Westmead was a lovely little interlude, but that was all it was. 'Real life' still beckoned. Nepalgunj waited.

A week after we re-booked the tickets, we discovered that I was pregnant again. It was quite unbelievable, particularly after all our struggles to conceive the first time around. So then we were back to the drawing board and it was a very confusing drawing board. This baby was due at Christmas. Should we again cancel our tickets and extend our time in Australia? My heart said yes. I felt the need to be near good medical care. I again thought it was God's answer, his 'hope for tomorrow'. Darren was not quite as convinced as I was, but he saw the toll it had taken on me and agreed that we needed to stay where we were.

We cancelled the aeroplane tickets. The following week, I miscarried the baby at eight weeks. The whole thing began again. More trips to the hospital. More doctors turning slowly around from their ultrasound screens. More needles. More beds floating away and more disappearing dartboards.

It's our heart that matters

During all this time, our supporters stayed faithful. They

prayed us through some difficult weeks. Our struggles became quite public. The nature of cross-cultural work means that a whole host of people know what you're up to. People from every state in the country are praying for you. People whose names you forgot three months ago are lifting you up to the Father on a daily basis. Because they were praying in detail, they wanted to know the details of our plans and as the days wore on that became harder and harder to share with them. We didn't know our plans ourselves.

One of the most faithful pray-ers was Jean Raddon. She had long been our 'hero in the faith'. Along with six other women, she had been part of the group of INFers who had walked into Nepal in 1952 when the country opened to the outside world. They began the Shining Hospital and saw the emergence of the first Nepali Christians. Her book describing those pioneering days, *Life on the Roof*, is an inspiring read. Along with Mary Miller, she has led a prayer group for Nepal that has met in their home for the last thirty years. Not one to ever retire, she founded Know Your Bible (KYB) for women in Australia and travelled around the world speaking to women and encouraging them in the faith. Jean would stand at the pulpit, knees bent, white hair thinning, eighty years of service having taken their toll. Then her voice would boom forth, 'Our God, he is AMAZING!' The hush would come over the crowd as this dear servant led women to understand the nature of our God who answers prayer.

Jean rang us at 8 a.m. one morning in early June. She had heard of our struggles and decided to pray through the night for us. If Jean had prayed through the night for us, then we needed to sit very still and listen.

'I'm as surprised by this as you will be,' she said. 'But I feel that God is saying to you to remain in Australia and finish your family. Our times are in his hands. He knows your heart and your desires to serve him so he'll honour those desires. But you have a long life ahead of you. You're young. There

will be a time to return to Nepal but now it's time to finish
your family. So be at peace in the knowledge that he cares for
you and he has something special for you for in this season.'

Jean's heart is all for mission. Sixteen years of service in
Nepal changed her forever. She would support cross-cultural
workers to the ends of the earth. For Jean to say 'stay' was
something extraordinary. She seemed to be as surprised by it
as we were. But she was convinced of the word in her heart.

It was a difficult season. We weren't immediately convinced
and we weren't particularly of one mind. Darren was still very
keen to return. He had left behind unfinished work. We had
both left behind friends who were waiting for our return. We
hadn't even said a proper goodbye. Of much lesser importance were all our belongings that were in the INF shed. It all
weighed very heavily. Then there were all the supporters who
were wanting to know our return dates.

Often in life, it can be very difficult to hear God say 'stay'.
You wouldn't think it would be. Why would it be so hard to
hear God say 'stay'? Isn't that an easy thing to hear?

I think for us, it was because our ears weren't attuned to it.
Our ears were getting blocked by the other sounds that were
forcing their way in – sounds of disappointment and sounds
of guilt. We were busy dwelling on what would have been to
the detriment of what was actually happening then. For me it
was a recurring refrain: if only the baby had lived, we would
be back there now with our friends. But the baby didn't live. I
needed to begin the long and exhausting process of clearing
my head of the unhelpful sounds, so that I could tune in to the
voice of God.

But even after sustained clearing, it was still hard to hear
God say 'stay'. I think it's just simply more exciting to hear
God say 'go'. The circumstances that surround 'go' are usually very positive. They're aching with the possibilities of service in a distant land where there are new friends to meet and

new cultures to understand and new opportunities to love the poor and the destitute. In contrast, the circumstances surrounding stay, for us, were negative. It was all about loss and sadness and uncertainty and confusion. It felt like a whole season of confusion.

We eventually decided to take two years' leave of absence from INF. That's the longest period you can take without having to go through the whole process of application again. Although things got better after we finally made the decision, we still felt very unsettled. I think the lack of leave-taking from Nepal compounded our grief and lengthened its resolution. For a long time we felt lost and directionless and as if we weren't really anchored anywhere. Our church was supportive but because we were only home temporarily, we had no role there. Darren was carrying on with his part-time jobs and I felt like running away, anywhere.

In July we became the managers at the short-term flats. That meant moving again and unpacking again. But this time after unpacking, there was more of a feeling of permanence. Two Korean families moved in and I began to teach English to the women. Unsurprisingly, I had a new heart for people arriving in a foreign land without language or understanding. I started taking the women shopping in Parramatta to practise their English. And the tables were strangely turned. Just a year earlier, I'd been the one feeling like I didn't really know what was going on around me. And I began to see that no experience in our life is ever wasted. God, the Lord of the seasons, uses it.

I decided, on another morning, that I would start looking for a job. I got myself up early and dressed well. I knew what I was going to do. I would go back to my old boss at Westmead and ask what was available. It was 8 a.m. and I was on my way out the door when the phone rang. It was her! We'd had no contact with her for years. But here she was on the very morning that I had decided to visit her, ringing me. She had rung to

offer me a part-time job at the Brain Injury Unit. It was two
days a week and quite perfect: a five-minute walk from our
front door, a case load that I would find manageable, and col-
leagues that I already knew. The work was available on the
days that Darren was available to mind Stephen. The Lord
prepares our paths.

Dal bhat in Sydney

He also prepares the people on our paths. One of the hardest
things in that season was that we missed our Nepali friends.
We missed their fellowship and their encouragement. We even
missed their three-hour-long church services. We were so sad
that we hadn't said goodbye. We wrote letters in Nepali, but it
wasn't the same.

But God was busy preparing the next thing. Unbeknown to
us, there were 5,000 Nepalis living in Sydney. A very small
handful of these had come to Christ and were meeting for fellowship on Friday nights. They met with a wider group at an
Assemblies of God church in Cabramatta on Sundays. We
made contact with them and walked nervously into the room
the following Sunday. Would we be able to speak Nepali in the
wrong context? How should we greet them? What if I get my
verbs wrong? But the first *Jai Masih* (Victory to Christ) put us
at ease. We were transported back to our other life of *dal bhat*
and time to spare and endless sitting around chatting, praying
and singing worship songs in Nepali – all in our own home
town.

Our new friends lived in tiny quarters in Marrickville, half
a dozen of them in one room, sharing a couple of chairs from
the local second-hand shop. They were working in factories
and sending all their wages back to their families in Nepal.
They were delighted to meet some locals who understood

them and who could speak their language. Even better than that was the fact that we could eat three plates of piled up *dal bhat* and still want more. Mind you, that was Darren. I always stopped at one and a half. The half was to show that I really did think it was incredibly *mitho* (tasty). We spent a great deal of time with them over the next few years and to this day are in awe over God's provision. Exactly at our lowest point he gave us what we needed.

A time to mourn . . .

It's easy to try and analyse a difficult season. At a human level we want to try and make some kind of sense of it. What did we do wrong? What was God really saying? Did we make the wrong decision? We even had some well-meaning friends ask us whether we thought our losses were a result of our disobedience. I couldn't agree. I think our God loves us and cries with us. He collects our tears in a bottle (Psalm 56:8) and he hurts as we hurt. His ways and his plans might be above our comprehension but his love isn't. And that's what he wants us to hold on to.

In some seasons, it feels like all we can do. In August I hung on again. I had fallen pregnant again and tentatively begun to hope that everything would be all right this time. I moved about the house very carefully. I hardly dared to sneeze. I was extremely careful lifting Stephen. I was probably a bit obsessed.

Then at 10 weeks I miscarried the baby and the distress was every bit as real as the other two times. I had the feeling that if I let myself have a really good cry I might never stop. Not only the bed we were sitting on, but the whole flat might float away – all the way down to the Parramatta River. So I tried very hard to keep it in. I tried to avoid meeting people who would ask me how I really was. Then, I tried to avoid telling people how I really was. But I hung on to God.

The other thing that I began to do during that season was to write down all the things he was teaching me. They were many. They were all about his purposes and his love for me. He was in control and he was at work in my life – and my response was to trust him. There was nothing I couldn't handle with him. There was nothing that I could go through which would be outside of his purposes. Everything in my life happens for two reasons: that he would get more glory and that I would be made more like him and be prepared for heaven. Lord, help me reflect your image more and more, I prayed.

It's easy to go through a great learning curve with God and then expect that he'll give you what you want. I felt like I did just that. 'Thank you for teaching me about your ways and about your love for me. I really have learnt it now and I'm ready for the next season. I really am ready *now* . . .'

But the next season wasn't due yet. I fell pregnant again. I miscarried our fourth baby in November at 8 weeks. You might think I would have been used to it by then but I wasn't. I cried and cried. I hung on again and he held me again.

Then one day I had a vision. I actually saw myself lying in the sun on a rock. I was obviously exhausted and there was no way I could get up. I couldn't even lift a finger, let alone a limb. And then it was like the Lord said to me very gently, 'Naomi, you've come to the end of your strength and you've got nothing left. So now I'm going to give you mine. I'm going to get you up and give you the strength you need but it will be mine, not yours. From now on, you operate in my strength and you live in me. That's what you came to this place for – and now that you've been here, you can love the others who come here. There are so many that come here and you'll be able to comfort them with the comfort I have given you.'

We each go through difficult seasons and in some of them

God feels distant and absent. Our prayers seem to bounce off the ceiling, if they even make it that far. 'Are you really there, God?' we ask. But in others of those difficult seasons, we're aware of an incredible sense of being upheld and loved and comforted. His presence is every bit as real as the people who share those seasons with us.

And I'm not sure what makes the difference. For me, the season of grief was one of being magnificently upheld. To this day, I look back on it as being a time of great intimacy with God. We didn't have long debates, I didn't pour out my thoughts or my questions. I didn't intercede or offer praise. I didn't try to figure out his plans for me. I hardly said anything at all. I just sat in his arms of love, hardly moving, hardly breathing but very aware of his comfort and love.

I wonder why I can't do that in the ordinary seasons?

It was such a relief when 1998 rolled around. We felt like we could put 1997 behind us and begin again freshly in a new year that hadn't known tragedy yet. Surely our year of drought was over? I began a two-year counselling training course with the Anglican Counselling Centre and it helped me more than I imagined possible. Darren began a diploma in theology at SMBC, which was exactly what he needed. We purchased a little house in the Blue Mountains and then rented it out for a short period. We weren't quite ready to move in yet.

I fell pregnant again! The 8-week scan was good, the heartbeat was strong. But at 12 weeks we discovered that we would again lose the baby – it wasn't viable. It was our fifth loss. The new year also knew grief. The seasons had merged again. Further tests showed that we needed to wait for six months before conceiving again. Amidst the heartache, we knew what we had to do. A six-month break meant that we could return to Nepal for a short period. One thing that the counselling course had shown me was how lacking we were in closure. We realised that we needed to draw the line on the previous season before we could begin the next. So we eagerly booked our tickets and kept telling Stephen how much fun it would be. He turned 3 and off we went.

Another adventure . . .

10

A SEASON OF CLOSURE
Pokhara, Nepal

Kathmandu in July 1998 was pretty awful. We took a little black *tuk tuk* to our favourite hotel and restaurant in Thamel, the tourist area of Kathmandu. Stephen happily carried the key up the last flight of crooked stairs and even managed the sticky lock in number 239. He rushed to the window and watched the pigeons gathering on the roofs below him. We looked around the grim walls of the hotel, mould creeping over the ceiling and threadbare bedspreads. We looked at each other. In our previous seasons in Nepal this hotel had been a treat, the epitome of luxury and escapism.

But not in this new season. I flaked out on the bed, stared at the mouldy ceiling and began to dream about all the other ways we could have spent the flight money, like a cruise in the Pacific or a skiing trip to New Zealand. We could have even gone to the UK to meet up with our old INF friends. But no, we were in Nepal. So we grabbed our bags and went out for breakfast to a bakery where we'd often gone for cinnamon rolls. They used to be delicious. That day they were stale and lifeless. Had the restaurant taken a major dive in quality? we asked. Or had we changed? Was our perspective that different? It was hard to know.

The next day we took the ten-hour bus trip to Pokhara and landed on the doorstep of our Australian friends. They had returned to Australia, as planned, for the birth of their second child and were now happily ensconced as a family in the life of the mission. I found myself watching them and thinking, this could have been us. We joined in their lives for a few weeks, we ate *dal bhat*, we even went trekking.

By then, Andrew and Sara had also returned from their honeymoon and moved to Nepalgunj. They met up with us in Pokhara and told stories of the new team and the work in that town; the one where we had thought we would live. We listened eagerly to their tales of God's provision and preparation and again we thought, it could have been us.

But nothing was quite the same. Even as I walked the streets of Pokhara, my heart response felt different. I watched women carrying their wearisome loads, their *dokos* full of grass cuttings, and knew that normally I would feel a burden for them. Normally, I'd want to reach out and connect with them in some small way; a smile here, a nod there or a quick chat. But this time I felt nothing and it really bothered me. Why was I so different? I wondered. Had I lost my compassion?

A time to uproot . . .

I slowly came to realise that it was the season. It was a season of closure, not a new beginning. In a season of closure we take time to say goodbye and to draw a line under what was before. I think God gives us what we need in order for us to do that. He doesn't give us a new burden for the people or fill our hearts anew with a desire to serve and love them. He lets us say goodbye. So that's what we did.

We moved down to a house very near our little old yellow house. Our Nepali friends came one by one to sit and chat and drink *chiya*. Shankar came first. He had married Bishnu Maya just before we left, a lovely girl from a nearby village. Their daughter Adipti turned out to be the sweetest thing we'd ever seen. Stephen thought so as well. They spent a lot of time playing hide-and-seek under the beds.

I remember Lalu coming. She looked older, but she had the same peace in her eyes. Saroj had returned from India but now he wanted to set up a prison ministry which meant he would be away a lot. Would she cope? We laughed and cried and prayed together. Then she read out from Psalm 139:23–24:

> Search me, O God, and know my heart; test me and know my anxious thoughts. See if there is any offensive way in me, and lead me in the way everlasting.

The same God who had been her rock for all those years would hold her close in the years to come. She was ready to trust him for the future.

So was I. We carried on with the task at hand. As well as lots of goodbyes, we also had to face the mountain of our belongings in INF's damp and dusty shed. Except that nearly two years had passed and what had started off being damp and dusty was now most definitely mouldy and musty. The monsoonal growth had almost covered the entry. While we were trying to forge our way through the rusty door, Stephen got stung by something nasty and ended up with a rash all around his neck.

It wasn't a good beginning. Actually it wasn't a good ending either. Most of our stuff was strewn all over the damp mud floor and we wondered why we had bothered keeping any of it. We passed most of it along to the next Australian INFer, lucky man that he was, and our clothes ended up on the backs of our Nepali friends. The Australians refused them . . . I'm not sure why.

Closure is never fun and it's certainly never exciting. We would probably all avoid it if we could. But we can't – not if we want to start the next season without baggage.

Interruptions

So we carried on with our goodbyes. As always happens, everyone wanted to see us again in the final days – a last *chiya*, a last *dal bhat*. Were we going to make it through? we wondered. Were we fitting everyone in? Time was running out and we were getting stressed. It had been a hectic and emotional time and we wanted to save the last days for our closest friends. But we kept being contacted by a lady called Ladli. She was a Nepali lady who we didn't know, we hadn't met and who we didn't particularly want to meet, but she was married to Binayak who was one of our Nepali friends in Sydney. In the last week, she rang every day to say that she would travel all the way up from Butwal (a six-hour bus ride) just to see us.

We relented. Perhaps we could fit in a breakfast *dal bhat* on the day before we left Pokhara. She was overjoyed. The next day she bounced in, accompanied by her father, and didn't seem to stop talking for the next two hours. A friendly chatty lady, she just wanted to talk about her husband. More than anything, she wanted to know about the new faith that Binayak had talked of since moving to Australia. 'Tell me all about it,' she said. 'Who is Jesus and why does Binayak believe in him? Is he different? Has Jesus made Binayak different and in what ways is he different?' The questions went on and on and we tried to field them as best we could.

The time passed and Ladli left carrying a Bible that we had given her. Seven years have passed since that day and we haven't seen her since. But on New Year's Day 2005, we were back in Nepal and Ladli rang to wish us a happy New Year. She told us that the word of God had changed her life. That very same Bible is with her all the time and she reads it daily. She takes it to church. The person who we thought was the annoying interruption was the one on God's heart. The one that we thought was a hassle or a blockage, was the one at the centre of God's plan. If only we could remember that in times of stress.

Hiding beneath a broom tree

We attended an INF service on our final night in Pokhara. The speaker used the story of Elijah in 1 Kings 18 and 19 to remind us of the tenderness of God as he ministered to an exhausted Elijah. Elijah had just witnessed a dramatic demonstration of God's power. So much so, that *all* the people . . . fell prostrate and cried, "The LORD – he is God! The LORD – he is God!"' (1 Kings 18:39). But Elijah was exhausted and fearful for his life so he hid beneath a broom tree, wishing he was dead. Then, the Lord gently touched him and provided him with food. He allowed him to sleep again before providing him with some more food. Only later did the Lord speak to Elijah and, when he did, it was in a gentle whisper. He gave Elijah new hope and offered him a way forward, saying, 'Go back the way you came, and go to the Desert of Damascus' (1 Kings 19:15). Then the Lord gave Elijah specific instructions for what to do when he got there.

I think he does the same thing in our lives. Very often in times of great trial, it may seem that he's silent. Yet when we come to the end of our strength God meets us at our point of need. Sometimes he meets our physical needs first. Perhaps we need rest and food. Sometimes he shows us the way forward. Whichever he does, he does it gently and quietly. Sometimes he speaks to us through his word, sometimes through the wise counsel of friends and sometimes through a still small voice in our hearts. And he gives us peace. As we left that service, we too had peace in our hearts.

'Go back the way you came,' was the word to Elijah. On that night, we knew that we were also ready to 'go back the way we had come'. We had said our goodbyes and closed off the season of our lives in Nepal. We were glad we had come.

Probably the most inspiring bit came at the very end of the trip. We were spending a few days in Kathmandu, on our way home. The only friends that we hadn't been able to meet during our time in Nepal had been Resham and Sita. They had again been targeted for their Christian activities and received warning letters that detailed threats on their lives and on the lives of their two sons. So, for the sake of the boys, Resham and Sita spent three months in hiding. Nobody knew where they were, not even the staff at the Bible correspondence course. Thinking it wasn't possible for us to meet them, we had given up. We would somehow try to write to them instead.

Then, on our very last day in Kathmandu, we received a cryptic note detailing their whereabouts and requesting that we come and see them. It seemed that their hideout was on the outskirts of the city, so we followed the directions and got in and out of numerous *tuk tuks*. Nobody was going to follow us, especially in that amount of rain and mud! We were not particularly relishing our fifth monsoon, but we were discovering that 3-year-old boys see the whole 'muddy thing' quite differently to how we do. Stephen was happy and so were we.

The last *tuk tuk* turned off its engine and we looked vaguely around us. We looked at the scene and checked for potential followers, as discreetly as we could. Around us there wasn't very much. There were a few run-down buildings separated by divots of mud and monsoonal growth. But after a while we noticed a movement to the left of us. The shadow of a head appeared in the bottom floor window of one of the buildings. The shadow turned into Sita. Resham was already at the door directing our entry.

The most difficult decision was what we should do first. Should we exclaim, sing, catch up, pray or eat *dal bhat*? Or all of the above. 'All of the above' won. It seemed that Resham and Sita, like Elijah, were also 'sitting under a broom tree'. But it was not a tree of their own making. Circumstances had forced them to sit under the tree and the Lord was there tenderly encouraging them and meeting their needs.

It was the first time in thirty years that Resham and Sita had taken a break from their work. They didn't have the word 'holiday' in their vocabulary. Most Nepalis don't. They had been involved in thirty years of non-stop evangelism and gospel work but now there they were forced to stay in one room. They had seen very few people for months. You would think Resham would be champing at the bit, but he wasn't. He was thanking God for the time to stop and dwell in him.

As we prayed together over the next hour, I felt very inspired by the way they were accepting and appreciating their season. I wished that I could learn from them and do the same. And then as we prayed some more, it was as if the next season was slowly moving into view, for all of us. We were sure that God had a purpose in our meeting that day. We stopped praying and looked at each other.

Darren spoke first, 'There are 5,000 Nepalis in Sydney. We could organise your stay. We have all the contacts. They're waiting for you – and you would be a labourer in a new harvest.'

Resham and Sita didn't need convincing. We exchanged contacts and said goodbye, all of us firmly convinced that we would meet up again in the next season, in a new country. And we did.

11

A SEASON OF NEWNESS
Blue Mountains, Australia

When you first step off the plane from the Third World and into Sydney, there are all sorts of things that strike you. The deep-blue sky reflects off the harbour and directs you to the high-rise skyline. Buildings made completely of glass dazzle your unaccustomed eyes. The clean, orderly roads meet in deliberate intersections, rather than in haphazard encounters. There's no rubbish heaped into sweltering piles and there are no beggars wanting handouts. There are no *tuk tuks* weaving in and out of the traffic. There's hardly any noise. Indeed, no one seems to be using their horn. And the traffic is going so fast. It's going so fast that it feels dangerous.

In August 1998 we gripped the edge of our seats as the speedometer crept up to 110 kilometres per hour. In Nepal we had been lucky to reach 40 kilometres per hour, and that was only when the buffalo gave us a clear run on our borrowed motor scooter. But now we were being hurtled down the highway as if we were an aeroplane on the runway. Any minute now we would take off. That would be us, a speck up there in the sky, zooming off into the distance. We stared out of the windows as if we expected them soon to be filled with clouds.

When the clouds didn't appear, we calmed down a bit and stared at the houses instead. We seemed to be passing through row upon row of inner city suburbs. There were immaculate houses with freshly clipped gardens. Every garden seemed to be bordered by a neat little fence and every fence had its gate firmly closed. There were no buffalo wandering in. Every curtain seemed to be drawn and every door seemed to be shut. We kept wondering where all the people were. We tried hard to spot one but they didn't seem to be part of the picture.

You can't go anywhere in Nepal without meeting people – lots of people. Their lives are lived outside on the streets, in the bazaar. The children play *carom board* and juggle their *chungi* with the inner part of their foot. The adults sit under Pipal trees and while away the hours, picking out nits and chatting to their neighbour. Actually, often they're not even chatting. It's more like watching – they're watching each other go by. When we first arrived in Nepal, Darren had to keep reminding me, 'Walk slower,' he said. 'We're not in a hurry, so perhaps we should just sit for a while.' After three years I think I actually got the hang of it. And I even enjoyed slowing down. I enjoyed just watching.

In Sydney, generally, people don't watch. They move really purposefully. It's particularly noticeable if you spend any time in the city centre. The crowds seem to know where they're going, they know why they're going there and they'll achieve it in another twenty-three seconds. Bags tucked under their arms, eyes focused, they march on. They look neither to their right nor to their left. They don't need to. There's no buffalo about to headbutt them or open sewer about to catch them. There's not even a holy man about to coerce them. They just move.

So did we. We moved out of Sydney and up into our house in the Blue Mountains. We thought that the mountain environment might lend itself to a slightly more relaxed pace, a more community feel and a more other-centred life. We were right in many regards. The Blue Mountains sit an hour to the west of Sydney and they form a natural barrier to the Greater Sydney Basin. Although many residents commute to the city, generally people who appreciate the quiet and the trees and the slower pace live there.

A time to gather stones . . .

We certainly appreciated the quiet and the trees. The little house that we had bought was situated in a quiet cul-de-sac, backing onto bush. It was a refuge. Our back yard was an immediate hit with Stephen. Complete with caves and water-falls and climbable trees, he thought he was in heaven. From the back patio we looked out over a tree-filled gully and dis-tant mountains. Well, they weren't quite the Himalayas, but they were nice.

The other thing that was nice was that it was ours. After spending the eight years of our married life in all sorts of strange rented accommodation, it was a wonderful feeling. One day we both walked into the living room and got annoyed with a door which didn't need to be there and thought, 'Hey, we can take a door off if we feel like it!' So we simply found the screw-drivers and took it off. Then we threw it under the house. We quickly got the hang of it and proceeded to knock down the laundry, the shed, the greenhouse, the front fence, the . . . whole back half of the house. No, actually that came later.

First of all we had to find two new jobs, a new church and a new preschool. At the base of the Blue Mountains is a large city called Penrith. Darren soon found himself in a thriving sports practice. He was back in his element, but he did admit early on that the patient who walked in with a 'slight twinge in his elbow if he threw a ball for two hours' reminded him that he was a long way from Pokhara. He was a long way from the life and death scenarios that had haunted him.

I found part-time work in the outpatient rehab section of Nepean Hospital and, again, it was perfect. Stephen found himself at a cute little preschool just down the road. We all found ourselves at a local church. That was a shock at first as well. We sat on chairs. Graham, our Pastor, would preach (in English!) for exactly twenty minutes. Not a minute more and not a minute less. Stephen went to Sunday school. He didn't have to spend three hours amusing himself on my cross-legged lap. We stood up at the end of the fifty-five minute service without feeling like our legs would fall apart. Surely it wasn't over already, we thought, we were only just getting going.

Trying to reconnect

Resettling permanently in Australia was actually very hard. Most people will tell you that the readjustments 'back home' are every bit as hard as the first cross-cultural move. And they take every bit as long.

At first it was the more superficial concerns. One day I walked into what I was sure used to be the post office. I waited in the line for a good twenty minutes. Finally I found myself at the head of the queue and I was about to ask for my set of twenty 45-cent stamps. I opened my mouth and . . . noticed that I was in a bank. My mouth somehow closed over the unarticulated words and my face felt terribly hot. I put my head down as far as it would go and managed to find my way back out through the throng and to the exit.

At the next shop, they inquired whether I had a store card or wanted 'FlyBuy' points. I had no idea what they were talking about. In my confusion, I handed over the money but accidentally did it Nepali style. I placed my left hand on my right elbow, turned my right palm to the ceiling and did a little bow. The man at the checkout squinted at me. Is she for real?

Even when you are only away for a few years, societies move on during that time. Answering machines, mobile phones and email all came in while we were away – which doesn't sound like a big deal, but it all added up to making us feel like we were strangers again; out of our depth and in the fog. What had become real and familiar to us was sitting on a stool in a little box-like shop as the *sahuji* (shopkeeper) carefully weighed out 2 kilograms of sugar and 5 kilograms of flour on her little scales.

But the superficial concerns can be overcome quite quickly. Through necessity I got the shopping down pat again. I figured out what was a bank and what was a post office and I learnt about FlyBuys. I kept my left hand in check while shopping and I stopped bowing.

But as soon as I got myself through that initial survival stage, other issues popped their heads around the corner. I struggled with what I perceived to be a lack of contentment in the heart of the average Australian. Friends would look around their ten-roomed house and deplore their lack of space or their unrenovated kitchen. I tried very hard to see life through their eyes. But no matter how hard I tried, I couldn't really connect. I couldn't forget Shankar.

Actually, a disconnected feeling followed us for quite some time. In Nepal, everything in our lives had a single goal, which was to serve the Nepali people with the love of Jesus. Our friends and contacts either shared that goal or were part of that goal, as was our work and church and all our activities. It was all connected but, in our new home, nothing seemed connected. Our work was separate to our church, which was disconnected to our social contacts. There didn't seem to be a common vision . . . or not one that I could easily lay hold of.

So instead we lay in our back garden. We drank in the fresh mountain air and watched the kookaburras as they spied on worms. We watched Stephen collect cicada shells. We built climbing ropes and tyre swings and tree houses. We dug up the earth and planted peas and beans and chillies. We had barbecues down on the 'big rock' (which formed the roof of the cave). We even ate *dal bhat* down there. We reconnected with old friends as well as making new ones and we gradually became rooted in our new home and life.

Then our old friends from Nepal arrived in Australia. The day that Resham and Sita came to stay at our house, our entire water supply was cut off. I think a pipe was blocked. They had just come off a twelve-hour flight from Nepal and we couldn't even offer them a functioning toilet. We laughingly apologised and I think they caught the joke. They probably decided that Australia was just like Nepal. They themselves had never lived anywhere with running water, so they seemed to enjoy it after the pipe was fixed.

Even more than the water, they enjoyed meeting all our Nepali friends in Sydney. Resham, ever the evangelist, soon had some big meetings organised. He preached to hundreds of Nepalis and Indians in Sydney's Inner West, in Newcastle, Tamworth and Wollongong. Many of them came to Christ. The Friday night Nepali fellowship grew and grew. The singing certainly improved. Resham taught them all his favourite Nepali worship songs and they caught on quickly. They couldn't stop.

One young girl who came to Christ was Puja. She had been married to a wealthy Nepali man and was brought to Australia to start their new life. But he had a tendency to vio-lence and life became miserable for Puja. Then one day he never came home. He had disappeared to Europe and found himself another girl. Puja was devastated. With no family around her and no job, survival was going to be a challenge. She couldn't afford to return to Nepal and she couldn't afford to stay in Australia. She certainly couldn't reveal her disgrace to her strict Hindu family who waited for her back in Nepal.

It was in this state that Puja turned up at a Nepali meeting organised in the inner city of Sydney. Resham was the preacher.

After the songs and sermon, a question time was held. It was surprising that this lady was asking so many questions and so boldly. 'Who is Jesus?' she said. 'How do you follow him?' 'How does he take away your sins?' 'How does he give you peace?' 'Would he do this for anyone, even me?' It's unusual for Nepali girls to speak up so confidently in public meetings and certainly not that boldly. She was obviously from an educated family.

She went away from the meeting with many new ideas to think through. She came to another meeting organised in Newcastle just north of Sydney. Along with a bus-load of Nepalis, she arrived full of anticipation. Again there were songs, a talk by Resham and then question time. Puja had obviously been thinking it all over and wanted to clarify her thoughts. She followed up her previous bombardment of questions with more. After the questions a time of prayer was held and this young lady had thirty Nepalis around her praying for her life. Through many tears she gave her life to Christ that morning and she experienced his peace for the first time. There was no easy way out of her problems but there was peace. And there was a new family.

After three months in Australia, Resham and Sita left for India. Their lives were still in danger in Nepal, but they thought they could work on the Nepal–India border safely. That way they could still reach Nepalis as they came in and out. We didn't want to say goodbye but we knew we had to. We would see them again we felt sure. We didn't know which country that would be in or which season it would be in but we knew that God knew. He knows all of our comings and goings, so we read together from Psalm 139:16:

> All the days ordained for me were written in your book before one of them came to be.

It's easy to read that verse and not really take it in. Perhaps it's become too familiar? Sometimes, the best passages become too familiar. I have to read them over and over again until they really sink in again. It was the case with that one. If all the days ordained for me were written in his book before one of them came to be, it means more than my time to be born and my time to die. It means every single day in between.

That could be each of the 29,200 days. It means the boring days and the chaotic days, the forgotten days and the painful days. They were written in his book – as are the memorable days. '*All* the days ordained for me were written in your book before one of them came to be.' All the days for Resham and Sita were also written in his book before one of them came to be. So we said goodbye.

How many days?

On one of those ordained days in 1999 I discovered that I was again pregnant, for the seventh time. Our new friends and acquaintances in the Blue Mountains were really excited for us. I tried to calm them down. 'No, no, no,' I said. 'You don't quite understand. I've had a few problems. The baby may not live.'

I think it was a coping mechanism. If I didn't get my hopes up, I might not crash so badly. If I didn't expect the baby to live, I might not fall apart completely if it died. If nobody else got their hopes up either, I might be able to pretend it didn't matter.

Actually, it's impossible not to get your hopes up when you're carrying a longed-for baby. My hopes went up as soon as I saw the line darken on the pregnancy test; as soon as I knew that there was another heart beating in there, another soul forming, with all of its days yet to unfold.

But how many days would there be? How was I to know? What if there were only a few? I moved into what became an extremely anxious season of life. It was marked by questions.

Everybody said, 'Try to stop worrying. You can't do anything anyway. Worrying never helps. It can make it worse . . .'

I knew that! But how could I stop worrying about it?

'Well, just try to stop thinking about it,' was their rational response.

Try to stop thinking about it . . . Try to stop thinking about it . . . I couldn't stop thinking about it. I was carrying my baby and I had just lost the previous five. Every waking moment, I was aware of the baby and I was thinking about him or her. I was worrying and wondering how I would cope if we lost it. I wasn't sleeping too well.

The night before the 18-week ultrasound was the worst. I hardly managed to close my eyes, let alone sleep. My mother was visiting and she was the first person who didn't tell me to stop worrying. She understood. Given what I'd been through, she said, of course I'd be worried. In hindsight, I think she was just as worried as I was. But it was nice to be given the freedom to simply 'be'.

The baby made it through the 18-week ultrasound. So did we. I didn't even pass out. I rediscovered what sleep was. Sleep was very good. More weeks passed uneventfully and I relaxed even more. Then, at about 32 weeks my doctor was concerned that the baby had stopped growing. Perhaps the same thing had happened to Stephen, which was why he'd been small.

So then we jumped up a level of worry as well as of activity. For the next five weeks I was always at Nepean Hospital having ultrasounds. I was always peering at them trying to figure out skull circumferences and femur lengths. I again lost sight of the rest of life. All I could think about was the life within me. The season took over.

Then at 37 weeks the doctor came to a conclusion: the baby had definitely stopped growing and needed to come out. I would have to be induced the next day.

That night I went into natural labour. And I discovered that it's a very simple process in the West. We had a phone. The phone worked. We rang the hospital and said we would be coming. We had a hot shower. It was very nice, very relaxing. We had a car. The car worked. We didn't have to push it. It wasn't raining. It was the clearest night. We rounded the last hill of the mountains and could see Penrith spread out before us. There was one single and very bright star sitting directly over Nepean Hospital! We smiled at each other. How lovely.

The hospital was just so comfortable and so clean. The tea trolley came round and I decided that, yes, I would quite like some breakfast. There were no other strange relatives sitting on my bed or on the floor. I didn't need to clamber over anyone and I didn't need to rewrite the childbirth manual. My gleaming surroundings looked just like those in the manual and so did the people. The people consisted of the midwife and an occasional doctor . . . nobody else. It actually seemed really quiet. There were no other fascinated onlookers jostling for positions in order to peer at the white girl.

The electricity didn't go off. I had my own toilet and it wasn't overflowing with unmentionable contents. It was so close. I think I was just enjoying the atmosphere. I was definitely in labour, but life is relative. Everything seemed so easy compared to last time. Painful, yes, but *easy*.

Just before lunch on 15 September, our second son arrived. He was alive and he was perfect. He was small and blonde and gorgeous. We named him Christopher. He weighed in at 1.9 kilograms . . . as if that's what babies always weigh. He was tiny. He fitted on the palm of Darren's hand. We couldn't stop staring at him. We couldn't stop loving him. I held him in my arms and thought about the love I was feeling. It's funny how the amount of love that we have to give, expands at exactly the same rate as our family does.

We had to stop staring though. In just a few minutes Christopher was whisked away to the neonatal intensive care unit. He was too tiny to suck and his blood sugars were dangerously low. He was soon fitted out with every possible tube and placed in a humidicrib. We sat there for long hours hunched over the box, taking in his little face and feeling thankful.

We couldn't help comparing the experience to our time in Nepal nearly four and a half years earlier. What had been the state of Stephen's blood sugars? How would we have known? As we dwelt on Christopher in the humidicrib, we became even more thankful for the life of our two sons. Christopher was here and he was OK. He was being looked after. Stephen had also made it, without the help of all the tubes and the technology. His survival now seemed even more of a miracle than it had at the time.

We were thankful and we remained that way for six whole weeks. We revelled in our new family. We spent a great deal of time watching both the boys, with hearts full of gladness. Once again, I wrapped up my baby in the blue bunny rug and filled up the empty curve in my elbow. He fitted perfectly. The emptiness had gone away. I still couldn't quite believe that we were four . . . after all this time.

But all too soon, only six weeks later, the next season was upon us. It was a season that we would never have expected and it arrived in the way that those seasons always arrive . . . with an incredible fright.

12

A SEASON OF FEAR
Blue Mountains, Australia

Darren is one of those all-round sportsmen. You know the type. No matter what sport he takes up, he excels at it. I've sometimes wished I had half his stamina, or half his co-ordination, or half his reflexes, or half his anything, for that matter. As well as reflexes and co-ordination, he has that other ingredient: the competitive edge. It drives him onward.

It started out with soccer. By the time he was 11, he was playing Youth League, which then led into the Federation Cup (state level soccer). At high school, he became the youngest player to be selected for our first-grade soccer team. I, a lovesick teenager, watched from the sidelines. Wow, I thought.

At 14, he took up squash. By the time we were at college, he was playing first-grade state squash and, at one stage, we even considered throwing in physio and heading off to Europe so that he could join the European squash circuit. We didn't, mind you, but we thought about it. He would regularly compete against the top players in Australia. When it was time for us to leave for India, he was at the peak of his squash career. He was playing extremely well. Three nights before we got on the plane, he played his last first-grade game. He won. Then he carefully wrapped up his squash racquet, packed it away in a box and never picked it up again.

I thought it would be hard for him. It had been such a major part of his life. You can't play state level anything without being just a touch obsessed. There were no squash courts in either India or Nepal so I worried about how he would cope without it and, more importantly, what he would do. He often talks now about that moment. When he put the racquet away, he says, it was like God gave him a new peace. He walked away and never thought about squash again.

In Nepal, he took up cycling. It was transport at first. He had to get us around town somehow. He happily transported me (on the rack) and then Stephen as well (on the front bar), all around the Pokhara Valley; through rain and mud, over dilapidated bridges and past acres of rice paddies. He discovered he liked it.

So then he took up triathlons. In those days, there was an annual Annapurna Triathlon run in our home town of Pokhara every January. It was a 2-kilometre swim across the lake, an 80-kilometre cycle up and over the nearest mountain, then a 20-kilometre run up and down that same mountain. He entered twice and came seventh both times. Mind you, the field wasn't huge, but he was doing pretty well.

Improving the training regime

When we returned to Sydney, he bought his first road bike and discovered Sydney's very smooth bike paths and breakdown lanes on the highways. He loved it. They must have felt incredible after Nepal's muddy paths and eroded lanes. He then started entering the half Ironman held in Canberra each year. It was usually run in February and consisted of the same distances that he had completed in Pokhara . . . but the mountains were much smaller.

One year, Mum and her partner Keith joined Stephen and me on the sidelines. We all watched Darren make the transitions and cheered him onwards. At the end of the race, Mum was concerned, 'He doesn't look very well,' she said.

I had a closer look at his face which did seem to be a bit grey. 'Well, he's just swum 2 kilometres, cycled 80 kilometres and run 20 kilometres. I suppose it's normal to look like that,' I said. I didn't give it another thought.

To improve his training regime, Darren bought himself a heart rate monitor. Knowing what his heart rate was, meant that he could push himself that little bit further. He could get more of the cardiovascular effect. It worked quite well at first, but then one day he came in from a run and threw it on the table in disgust.

'The monitor's gone on the blink! How frustrating, I've only just bought it.'

I looked up from the newspaper. 'What's wrong with it?'

'It keeps doing the same thing. Whenever I get up to 130 beats per minute, it either goes off the screen or it jumps up to 230 beats per minute. Then, it goes even higher or it goes off the screen. It doesn't seem to work at all.'

In frustration, he packed up the monitor and sent it off to the company in Adelaide, with a note describing its errors. He wanted it fixed or he wanted his money back.

Some weeks later, he got the monitor back with a little note attached to it. 'Dear Sir,' the note read. 'We have given the monitor a thorough test in all ranges and we're confident that it works well. There are no alterations required.'

He tried it out again. 'What do you mean, "there are no alterations required"?' He did a short run through the bush and over the ridges near our house. No sooner had he reached 130 beats per minute, than the same thing happened. The monitor shot up to 230 beats per minute, flickered for a while and then went blank. There was nothing registering.

He arrived home very frustrated. 'They don't know what they're doing in Adelaide,' he said. 'If that's the case, I just won't wear it.'

Darren is not only an accomplished sportsman (and a wonderful husband), he can also be a touch stubborn at times.

It was winter in the Blue Mountains. That means there was frost on the ground and the mornings were freezing. Darren doesn't particularly like winter. Give him tropical heat and humidity and he's in his element. He feels good and he can get out and do all the things he wants to do, like run up mountains. In 40-degree heat, though, while he runs up mountains, I flake out under the fan.

But during the winter of 1999, he would come in from his runs and collapse at the kitchen table. 'I don't know why I feel so terrible,' he would say. 'Am I just cold? Have I forgotten how to run?' He wasn't sure.

And this went on for a while. Eventually, he decided he'd go and see his GP. That was a big step for him because he *never* sees a GP if he can avoid it. And the GP wasn't altogether helpful, 'Of course you're tired,' he said. 'You run a long way. It's normal.'

But Darren wasn't going to be put off. 'I think I need a stress test,' he said. 'I may even need a referral to see a cardiologist.' The GP eventually gave in, thinking it was a waste of time.

The referral letter lay on our kitchen bench for three months. It was the same time that Christopher arrived so we were fairly busy traipsing up and down from the neonatal intensive care unit. Even when Christopher did make it home, life was rather full. Tiny babies are a full-time job no matter what country you're in.

Too great a risk

On 1 November, Christopher was 6 weeks old and Darren went to see the cardiologist. He rang me from the clinic. I was holding the cordless phone and walking into the bedroom.

'Nom, they say I have to go straight to the hospital. I need an operation. They say it's very serious . . .'

'Hang on . . .' I said and sat down on the bed. 'Sorry? Say that again?'

'It's my heart,' he said. 'I have a ventricular tachycardia. It's an arrhythmia arising in the ventricles and it's very serious. I have to go straight to the hospital. I can't come home.'

'You can't come home,' I repeated inanely. 'Why can't you come home?' I wasn't getting it.

'Because it's serious.'

'What do you mean by serious?'

Darren put the nursing sister onto the phone and she repeated the same information. She said they weren't quite sure how Darren could be still alive. He would need an operation as soon as possible and, in the meantime, he needed 24-hour cardiac monitoring. It was far too great a risk to send him home. Anything could happen.

This was my 33-year-old triathlete husband. All of a sudden it was too dangerous for him to get in the car and drive home. Actually, he'd been planning on running home. The day before, he'd done an easy 10-kilometre run and yet, today, he needed 24-hour cardiac monitoring. It moved out of the realm of the possible.

It wasn't the monitor that was malfunctioning, it was Darren. It wasn't the monitor that needed alterations, it was Darren. All that time, he'd been running through a ventricular tachycardia (VT), registering well over 230 beats per minute and probably a lot more. The cardiologist didn't think it was possible. How was he still alive? Why hadn't he gone into fibrillation and arrested? He should have done. And how had he done five-hour triathlons through a VT?

It was better not to think about it. I gathered the boys and we made our way down to Nepean Hospital once again. But we didn't visit the NICU. We went straight to the cardiac ward on level 5 and we found Darren hooked up to an ECG and confined to his hospital bed. His every move was being monitored by the sisters at the nursing station. It was unthinkable.

Stephen didn't get it either. 'Are you sick, Daddy?'

'No, mate, I'm not sick. I just have a funny heart.'

Darren had a three-hour operation the next day. It was just an exploratory one, to try to map the arrhythmia. An arrhythmia is an extra electrical pathway in the heart, which overrides the normal pacemaker. How big was it? Where was it? The location would determine whether they could try to ablate it, or whether they would have to put in a new artificial pacemaker. Nothing was certain.

Even after the operation, nothing seemed certain. All sorts of medical personnel put their heads together and conferred. They weren't sure. They would keep him in hospital and strictly monitored while they thought about it. And that began another week or so of traipsing to and from Nepean Hospital, this time to the cardiac ward. And this time with a tiny newborn as well as a 4-year-old, and no husband.

During that week, I received an airmail letter from Linda, my lovely INF friend who was now back in the UK: 'You must all be having such a wonderful time now that the four of you are all together. After all the waiting, you can sit back and enjoy your precious family. I can just picture you as you spend these special weeks together.'

I read the letter and cried. We had our longed-for second son, but we weren't sure whether we had Darren.

Back at the hospital, he was still restricted to his hospital bed and it was a hard time for all of us. After a lifetime of high-level training, he was told not to move. And the hard thing for him was that he didn't *feel* any different to how he'd felt the week before. But the staff kept telling him to stay completely still. He wasn't even allowed to do a push-up. It was too great a risk.

So he read and prayed. And after some days, he said to me, 'You know, I'm ready to go home. If that's what God wants,

I'm ready. I know that he's in charge and I'm OK with that. It's just that I don't want to leave all of you. How could I leave you?'

I looked back at his face and tried to stop the tears welling up. 'Mmm . . .' was all that came out.

A new fear

By 5 November I was exhausted. Christopher seemed to be feeding non-stop, in the way that tiny babies do. Stephen was stressed with all the hospital visits and so was I. I remember that we'd found something for lunch. I'm not sure what it was but we ate it. It was two o'clock.

Michelle arrived at the door. There's nothing quite like friends that you've had since you were 12 years old. They know you inside out. They've already seen the best and worst of you, so nothing can surprise them about you and nothing can surprise you about them. Michelle is one of those. She also has this knack of showing up exactly when she's needed.

'Right,' she said, walking through the door and immediately taking charge. 'Nom, you're going to sleep in here.' She was already pulling the curtains closed, 'And I'm going to take the boys out the back to give you a rest. And no matter what, you're not going to wake up till I say you can. Have you got that?'

I was already under the covers and asleep before my head hit the pillow. I didn't even stop to wonder what she'd done with her own two boys. I just slept. I didn't even turn over. I didn't hear the phone call.

But I sensed that she'd come back into the room. She sat down on the end of the bed and looked at me. I thought there were tears in her eyes.

'Nom, do you know where your dad is?' she said.

'No. I've no idea. Why?'

'You've just had a phone call from someone called Patricia,' she said.

'Patricia who?' I said, still half-asleep.

'I wrote it down. It says here. Patricia Pearse.'

'Oh. That's my aunt,' I said, 'Dad's brother's wife.' I leaned up on my elbow and looked at her. What would Patricia want? We hardly ever heard from Dad's relations.

Michelle took a deep breath. 'She said that your dad's been on a climbing holiday in Victoria. But there's been a terrible accident and he's had a fall. He's been airlifted to a hospital in Melbourne. They think he's broken his back. Patricia says it's very bad . . . he may not make it.'

I looked at her uncomprehendingly, 'My dad?' I said.

My dad was almost as invincible as Darren. At 58, he was still doing some elite-level climbing. He was in peak condition. He ran every day. He couldn't possibly be in hospital.

I sat up and looked at her again. 'What did you say?'

The poor thing; she'd come over to give me a two-hour sleep, not to be the bearer of bad news. But she started all over again. She knew the name of the hospital and what ward Dad was in. She even knew the name of his doctor. She had all the phone numbers ready for me. She gave me a big hug.

I felt numb. I was already on an overload of fear. Every nerve was already as taut as it would go. Perhaps I was a guitar and any minute now I would twang into a ball of tangled wire. I couldn't risk turning my head, let alone facing a new fear. I certainly couldn't face a new fear that was lying in another hospital, in another state, in another critical condition.

But I had to risk becoming the ball of tangled wire. There were no other options. I rang the number and spoke to his doctor. They wouldn't know anything for another few days. It was touch and go.

Two days later, I rang again. Dad was still alive but the diagnosis had been confirmed. He had become a T8 paraplegic. He had no sensation or movement below his nipples. He would never walk again, let alone run or climb. They would air-ambulance him back to Sydney when he was medically stable but it would be a long, slow process. They needed to fix the fracture site. He was in a lot of pain.

I had turned my head and faced the new fear but I couldn't do anything else. I couldn't leave Darren. My brother Tim flew down to Melbourne.

Meanwhile, back at Nepean Hospital, the doctors had made a decision. Darren needed a major operation. He needed an ablation of the pathway, which was a very tricky operation and could only be done at Westmead Hospital. And Westmead had a waiting list. So they suggested to Darren that he should come home to rest while he waited for his spot at Westmead. They said that as long as he did no exercise whatsoever, he should be all right. But he would have to be very careful not to do *anything* that would cause a rise in his heart rate.

The first day back at home passed quite uneventfully. It was lovely to be all together again. Darren walked slowly from room to room. He sat down a lot. He cuddled the boys and they cuddled him. And we all kept a constant eye on his heart rate monitor which stayed nice and low – nothing over 80. And we started to breathe again. We even took our eyes off the monitor for very short periods, maybe a whole minute at a time.

An outing

We both have a tendency towards optimism. By the second day, Darren was feeling good. The low numbers on the moni-tor had reassured him and he was starting to try and make sense of it, 'You know, my heart rate only ever went really high when I was exercising pretty hard. It only ever went off the screen after I got to 130 beats per minute,' he paused. 'Which means I'm perfectly safe as long as I stay under 130.'

I could tell by the tone of his voice that he was up to something. He was hatching a plan. He kept speaking, 'We could go out you know . . . We could take Stephen to the Sydney Aquarium. We've never been there and he'd love it. It's a good opportunity. We hardly ever get this amount of time off together. We should make the most of it . . .'

I argued for a while. But in the end I thought he had a point. It was true, he had never had a problem when he wasn't exercising. It would be an easy train trip into the city and then a slow walk down to Darling Harbour. What could be the harm in that? Stephen was also feeling cooped up and we could all do with a change of scenery.

The train trip was lovely. We watched out the window as the ridges of bush gave way to the flat plains, the river on one side and the highway on the other. Neat little houses surrounded by neat little parks and neat little shopping centres. Then further in, the factories and the industries, the smells of the city. Stephen had his nose pressed to the window. The harbour came into view, sparkling in the sunshine. The seagulls were soaring. The sailing boats were enjoying the calm of the day.

We quietly got off the train and walked slowly and carefully down the hill towards Darling Harbour. Christopher was asleep in his pram. Stephen was happily pointing out a man with a funny hat on. Every few steps, I looked down at the monitor. It was reading 90. That was OK. That was good. There was room to move.

And then we passed a pub on the corner of a main intersection and I looked down at the monitor again. It read 234.

Darren must have noticed it in the same instant. He sat down as calmly as he could . . . on the pavement. I don't remember the next few seconds. I was in the pub, calling an ambulance. I couldn't even tell them where I was. I didn't know. I looked out the door. What if he died while I was in the pub? Some kind man saw my distress and took over. I ran back out. He was still alive. Neither of us dared to move. Where was the ambulance?

'We're in Darling Harbour,' I said. 'This place must be loaded with ambulances. Where are they?!'

It came, screaming around the corner. The men came out and carefully put him on a stretcher and carried him inside. I said goodbye, my eyes wild. The ambulance started up again, the siren wailed and I watched until it turned the corner and disappeared out of view. I kept staring in the direction it had gone. I didn't move. I was frozen.

When I came to, I found myself with my two boys standing bereft on a corner of Darling Harbour, with no plan. Christopher was still asleep in the pram. Stephen had that look on his face, which meant that he was about to ask me at least a hundred questions. They were probably all relevant. I had some myself, like, 'What shall we do now?'

What indeed? I hadn't even checked to see whether I had any money on me. Often, only one of us carries money when we go on outings. I dug around in my bag and fumbled with the nappies and spare clothes. My hands groped about in that panicky manner that usually means they find pockets of air. In the middle of my fumbling, I also realised that I didn't even know where they'd taken him. Central Sydney has its fair share of hospitals. Which one had they disappeared to?

Despite living in Sydney for most of my life, my understanding of the geography of the inner city is fairly vague. Actually, my understanding of the geography of pretty well any location is pretty awful. I'm one of these dreamers who struggle to take in the details of life around me. I certainly wasn't going to be able to manage public transport at a time like this, especially to an unknown destination.

I needed a taxi . . . a big one, immediately, with a baby cap-sule and room for a pram. But I didn't know how to get an immediate, large taxi in Darling Harbour. I think the helpful man must been hovering around because someone phoned for a special taxi and it turned up. The whole period remains a blur – a bit like I was living someone else's life. The real me surely couldn't be chasing an ambulance through inner-city Sydney, with my husband inside it. I must have been watching someone else's life unfold . . . a terrifying life.

It's hard to catch ambulances. They go extremely fast. We decided to check out Royal Prince Alfred Hospital first. I did-n't even stop to ask at reception. There was no time. I defied all emergency room rules and pushed my pram through the busy section, Stephen keeping a good pace behind me. I even flung open cubicle curtains, desperate to find him, terrified that it would be too late.

He was lying in a bed behind curtain number seven, hooked up to more cardiac monitors, as calm as anything and proba-bly wondering why I was looking so wild. 'What's wrong?' he said.

I told him that I didn't want to ever go through that again.

The doctors at RPA eventually let him out with instructions to *bed rest.* 'That means bed rest!' they said. They told us to make our way home slowly and wait for the surgery appoint-ment at Westmead. And we weren't allowed to have any out-ings *anywhere*!

Hyper alert

For the next three weeks we role reversed everything . . . absolutely everything. Darren watched from the sidelines as I trimmed the biggest tree in our back yard. He sat under the fan.

The hardest thing was that it was essential that he remained calm. Any rise in his heart rate could be fatal. So he spent lots of time practising his relaxed breathing and that was fine for him. But on the other hand, it was essential that I remained alert. While Darren's heart rate stayed quiet and slow, mine was hitting all-time highs. For me, it was 'fight or flight' every minute of the day.

I reviewed my CPR and put the chart on the fridge. I kept fiddling with our emergency phone numbers which were always in my pocket. Every now and again I would pull the scrap of paper out, just to check it was still there. And it was. The numbers were a bit crumpled, but still legible. Then I'd go and check that the phone was still there as well.

But it wasn't just the days that had me on hyper alert. I think the nights were even worse. I'd turn over every few minutes and check his sleeping body. Then I'd try and pull his arm out from underneath him, slowly and carefully, so as not to wake him, and then read the wrist monitor. The moonlight shone in through a gap in the curtains and revealed the number – 75. Then I'd slowly breathe out and relax back onto the pillow.

I kept the pace up for three weeks. For the first time in our lives it was me who was having the training effect. Being on hyper alert was exhausting and all-consuming. There was almost nothing else entering my mind. I had no other thoughts. I didn't wonder how any of my friends were. I didn't ring anyone or think about what we would do the following week . . . if there was one. I just stayed in the moment, watching Darren's heart rate. Apart from feeding the boys, which was on autopilot, that was all I did.

And again, I hardly spoke to God. A few 'HELP's escaped from my mouth at various points during the day but that was all. It was quite a different season. During the season of grief, I'd been aware of the Lord holding me and comforting me. But during the season of fear, I was aware of nothing. It was pure moment-by-moment survival. I don't doubt in any way that he was there. His being present with me has absolutely nothing to do with my awareness of him. God is there, because he is there.

But perhaps that's simply how it is in a season of fear. I don't at this stage want to go through another one in order to find out. I'm still feeling drained just writing about the last one, but I know that we will all experience fear again at some stage or other. My prayer is that once we get to the end of it, when we're able to draw breath again, we'll draw on his mercy and kindness and grace.

Going deeper

After three weeks, the hospital rang to say that Darren's operation had been booked for Monday 5 December. He was admitted the day before. It was Sunday, so I stayed at home with the boys and went to church. I don't remember any of the service. I was probably trying not to think too hard. Just get through it. Don't think about tomorrow.

At the end, Graham stood slowly and announced the closing hymn. It was, 'Great is Thy Faithfulness'. I turned my book to the correct page and looked at the words. I knew them. I knew them well. But on that Sunday, I wondered whether I would be able to stand up and sing them. I wavered. I read them again. I wasn't sure.

It's all very well to sing 'Great is Thy Faithfulness' when you can see evidence of his faithfulness all around you; when his blessings and mercies seem to abound. But it's a whole different story trying to sing it when all you can see is fear, especially when those fears are about to overwhelm you.

The questions kept me on my seat. What if Darren didn't make it? What if God's mercies weren't evident in the morning? Everybody else was on their feet. Their bodies were merging into straight lines around me and I was still wavering. I was staring at the words and wondering whether they would come out.

If Darren died in the morning, would I still sing to my God, whose compassions never fail? Would I still sing to my God, who gives me everything I need? The answer was very slow in coming but when it did, it came from deep within.

Yes, I would. So I stood and sang.

The next day, I sat and waited. I waited for eleven hours, while a large medical team worked on him all day. Darren's dad, Dennis, was minding the boys so I sat in the hospital tearoom and wrote sixty-five Christmas cards – all the time wondering whether we'd be celebrating it. Just two days before, a friend had asked Darren if he would be around for Christmas. He said that he wasn't sure and they thought he was joking . . . but he wasn't.

When life hangs in the balance, all sorts of things become clearer than they normally are. Why am I here? For what purpose? What am I living for? And who holds my life in their hands? It's often been said that when it's our time to go, there's nothing on earth anyone can do to keep us here. Alternatively, if it's not our time to go, there's nothing on earth that can happen that would take us away.

I believed it at a head level. Head levels are easy. You just pack in the truth, nice and tight, so it doesn't move around when you shake it. But the heart level is different altogether. It shakes. What if it was Darren's time to go? Would I be able to bear it?

In a season where everything feels like it's falling apart, it's time to go deeper into the things of God. Maybe the only good thing about those kinds of seasons is that the truth that is normally out of reach becomes the truth that we're living by. We start to hang onto those things which are eternal and outside of time because all the other things that we normally hang onto have been taken away. It can be good to look carefully at what it leaves.

Before the beginning of time, God chose us (Eph. 1:4). He gave us his grace in Christ Jesus (2 Tim. 1:9) and he loved us. If those things are outside of time, it means that they're true yesterday, today and forever. They're present today and they'll be present until the end of time, no matter what.

> Who shall separate us from the love of Christ? Shall trouble or hardship or persecution or famine or nakedness or danger or sword? . . . For I am convinced that neither death nor life, neither angels nor demons, neither the present nor the future, nor any powers, neither height nor depth, nor anything else in all creation, will be able to separate us from the love of God that is in Christ Jesus our Lord. (Romans 8:35–39)

When we go through a season where we stare death in the face, we learn new things and we see new things and we believe new things. We hold onto the eternal and we find that it's enough.

Eleven hours later, Darren was wheeled back in to the cardiac ward from the operating theatre. The pathway had been ablated. No pacemaker was required and no further damage had been done. He was alive.

Ten per cent of all arrhythmias recur within the first six months. He still had to be careful. The following May we went back to Westmead Hospital and Darren underwent a third major operation to check that the problem hadn't recurred.

It hadn't. He was officially cured and the season of fear was officially over – seven months after it had started.

It took me a lot longer than seven months to calm down though. While I was still calming down, my dad moved out of

Prince Henry Hospital and into a halfway house for spinal cord injured patients. We would go out to the local park and he would show us his new wheelchair tricks. I panicked one day when he fell out. I mean, I *really* panicked. That was when I realised how jumpy I still was.

I think it's OK to take a long time to recover from seasons. After a while, they become part of our story and we seem to be able to integrate them. We can talk about them without too many autonomic reactions going on and we can even write about them.

But that doesn't mean that we've completely recovered. I'm now kinder to myself. I treat myself with more grace. If I find that I'm overreacting to a threatening situation, I take time to think about where I've been. And I remember that the Lord has been there with me. He understands the seasons I've been through and he was there with me. So if he understands and treats me with grace, then perhaps I should also be kinder to myself in the season at hand.

13

A SEASON OF DISTRACTION
Blue Mountains, Australia

The next season certainly helped me to calm down. It was a bit like watching an escapist movie on an aeroplane. It was very nice, very engrossing and even all-consuming at times. We renovated the house.

The only trouble was that 'renovating the house' was on our list of all-time *never do* activities. We'd written the list in Nepal when we were back there for closure and we'd spent time working out what our priorities would be for the next five years. We wrote down all sorts of good things that we wanted to do and then we wrote down about six things that we would never do.

One of them was to have a pet. We read that affluent Australians spend more money each year on their pets than the nation does on foreign aid. Apparently, the pets cost around $2.2 billion dollars each year and foreign aid spending was less than $2 billion. We were determined not to be a part of that. Not yet anyway.

Another no-go area was sending our children to private schools. We still haven't succumbed. Close, but not quite.

Then there was the little matter of renovating the house. It wasn't that we actually had anything against renovating. It was just that the letters we received from Australia while we were in Nepal seemed to be full of it. While we were dealing with the problems of poverty, people in Sydney seemed to be dealing with the excesses of wealth. Actually, it seemed that nobody we knew in Australia was doing anything but renovating their kitchens and bathrooms.

So we decided that we didn't want to become that distracted. We wanted our living to be deliberate. I remember a speaker at Reachout (a big missions convention) asking the audience, 'If Jesus had a spare $50,000 would he renovate his house?' Well . . . no, we thought, probably not. We weren't going to let ourselves become engrossed by such an all-consuming activity.

A time to build . . .

Two years later, we renovated the house – very quietly at first. We started off quite small with a picket fence. That couldn't hurt. It was just a weekend's entertainment. Then we replaced some windows. The old ones were broken and letting in the whistling mountain winds. It was a very cold winter. Then, a few more walls seemed to be randomly in the way. We knocked them down. After that, the floors needed polishing because surely clean floors would be better for the children, especially Christopher who was by then hauling himself along the floor, like a beached fur seal. And a back deck, the length of the house . . . now that would be good.

In renovating, one thing always leads to another, doesn't it? A nice new window makes the door look out of place. A freshly painted wall makes the flue look unfinished. A nice new basin makes the bath look old and worn. Changing a few simple walls means the whole roof needs redoing. You never seem to get that 'I'm finished' sort of satisfaction. The next job is already calling you.

By the time we were almost done (nearly two years later) the whole back end of the house had been demolished and rebuilt. The kitchen had become the bathroom. The bathroom had become the dining area. The dining area had become the kids' room. The kids' room had become the dining area. The patio had become the kitchen. Actually, nothing kept its original function.

The sunsets

It's easy to try to justify your actions when you find yourself doing something that you said you *never would*. We could think up any number of wonderful reasons why we were now spending so many spare moments renovating the house. Some of them were good reasons. We would be able to use the house for more entertaining. We could accommodate more guests. We were being accountable with what we'd been given. We were putting it to good use.

'But why are you *really* renovating the house?' a friend asked. It was a balmy evening and we'd just finished dinner so it was one of those relaxed moments where genuine responses can worm their way out. I looked across the table at him and realised he wasn't being judgemental in his question. He and his wife had just spent the previous seven years renovating their inner-city terrace so his question was merely a friendly inquiry.

And I answered with the first thing that came into my head. 'Because I want to watch the sunsets,' I said. A slight pause and then it clicked for me. Aha! I smiled to myself. The truth is out, just when I was so delightfully having myself on. It's got nothing to do with entertaining and visitors and using what we have for God's glory. It's got to do with sunsets.

When we bought our little house in the Blue Mountains, the thing that appealed to me most was its setting. The back garden faced west and backed onto acres of unspoiled Australian bush. A glorious array of knobbly red Angophoras, wispy Casuarinas and silver-backed Eucalypts stretched all the way down to a convoluted creek. On the way down, the adventurous amongst us discovered that these splendid trees actually concealed caves and waterfalls, cliffs . . . and leeches.

If we stood on the back patio, we could see over the gully to the distant blue hills. On calm mornings, flocks of white cockatoos would wing their way into our valley, calling to each other as they settled in our trees. On calm evenings, the cockatoos would depart into the sunset. They became specks of white, scattered through the reds and golds of the sky, framed by the trees and the blue hills. It was a picture.

But it was a picture that we couldn't see from inside. Whoever designed our house in the 1950s hadn't given any thought to its aspect. Along the entire back section of the house there was only one small window so you couldn't sit inside and gaze outwards at the view. You couldn't see the trees or the birds or the blue hills or the sunsets. You couldn't see anything at all.

From the inside, I knew that they were there. I could hear the birds calling and the cicadas answering, but I couldn't see them. I could smell the wild flowers and the Eucalypts, but I couldn't see them. I knew that it must be time for the sunset but I couldn't *see* it.

And that was the point. So by the time we were done with renovating, the resulting floor plan was a sea of windows. There were hardly any walls. We hadn't even succeeded in making the house any bigger. Actually we'd lost a bedroom . . . but we could see the view.

Arms that are full

I seem to keep saying *we* renovated the house. Darren would tell you that that's not entirely true and he's quite right. I did precious little. I painted a few token walls, held and passed some necessary tools, if I was nearby. At one point I did actually hold up the roof when there was a sudden flash flood, but that's about it. Darren renovated the house.

I was busy being what you might call 'otherwise occupied'. The renovation magazines that recommend you not to combine babies and renovations are probably quite insightful. By June 2000, Christopher was 9 months old and the renovation was well under way. That's precisely when I fell pregnant for the eighth time. The eighth time!

Even I had to keep repeating that phrase to myself as I stared down again at the faint blue line. I must have stared at it for a good long time. I leant my body up against the vanity and, as I did so, the other seven occasions passed dimly through my mind.

They passed dimly through, made their presence felt and then departed, leaving me to my moment of speechlessness. Then my eyes cleared and focused again. I looked up at the boys and the state of our home.

The kitchen was a shell. Even the plasterboard was gone. A couple of taps protruded from the wall, unwanted, not required. They were waiting patiently for their moment when they would be transformed into a bathroom. Meanwhile, the temporary kitchen was in the boys' room. The billy was once again on the boil. The water was once again being collected in buckets from the garden. It was my season of preparation all over again.

But it was a season of preparation that now included the kids, and that made it trickier. I well remember the day I lost concentration momentarily and I turned around to find Christopher with his bottom, feet and hands planted on the concreted floor that was to become the base of the new bathroom. It had just been freshly covered with wet fibreglass for waterproofing. He couldn't move at all. His hands, his feet and his bottom were all stuck in the stickiest, gooiest gunk you've ever seen. Stephen was the only one of us who saw the funny side of it.

Shortly after that there came a point where we decided the house was no longer habitable. Perhaps it was the gunk episode? So we moved around the corner and shared a house with Dennis, Darren's very generous and accommodating father. It was during those three months that the next utterly delightful, and distracting, event occurred. Our third son, Jeremy, was born.

You would have thought that given our experience of the previous seven pregnancies, there would be a gripping story here. To be honest, there isn't really. He seemed to appear while our backs were turned, in that enchanting and cheery way that he has lived life ever since.

In lots of ways it was similar to Christopher's arrival, except that the doctors had figured it out this time. I had a major problem with my blood flow, they said, which was why we had such troubles with pregnancy loss and low birth weight babies. They told us that there was every chance that this one would also either die *in utero* or stop growing at some point and need to be induced.

But they were on the job this time. The weekly ultrasounds started even earlier and, once again, we were peering at head circumferences and femur lengths. The anxiety built slowly as well.

Then, at exactly the same point, 37 weeks, the same pronouncement was made. 'The baby has definitely stopped growing. It's not safe for it to stay there. You'll need to be induced tomorrow.'

I went home, feeling quite calm and sure that it would happen that night. And it did. We slipped out quietly (resident babysitters are wonderful), and made our way back to Nepean Hospital. But I knew what to expect this time. I was going to make full use of the facilities. I rested back in the large water bath of the newly furbished maternity ward and didn't even think about re-writing the manual – I just enjoyed it! That's how far away we were from the WRH days.

The next day, 14 March 2001, at lunchtime, Jeremy made his way into our family, breaking all records. He tipped the scales at 2 kilograms. He was simply gorgeous. His tiny little face was framed by wisps of blonde hair. His round eyes peeped out at us from the folds of the blue bunny rug. We stared and we cuddled. We couldn't keep staring though; no sooner had he arrived, than he also made full use of the facilities. He was whisked off to the NICU and hooked up to every possible tube. His blood sugars were dangerously low and he was too tiny to suck, but I was an old hand now. I knew exactly what to do. I'd already expressed my first bottle of milk before the nursing sister even figured out what bed I was in.

Being that tiny bit bigger, Jeremy only stayed in the NICU for a week, so we both made it home together. Mind you, 'home' was not expansive. We were all sharing a single room in Dennis's house, but it was wonderful. All the curves in my elbows now felt unmistakably full, eight years after I had noticed they were empty. They not only *felt* full, they *were* full.

They were so full that I could hardly even carry everyone around the corner to check on the progress of the renovation. For the first time in my parenting I decided that prams were useful and so were grandparents. I also noticed that there's a way to speed up the renovation process. And that is to squash five of you into one room indefinitely, especially when one of the five is the kind of newborn that makes his presence felt at every opportunity.

Six weeks later we moved back into our house. I could see out of the windows. From every window there was now a glorious view of our waving gum trees and the gully beyond. I sat there contentedly feeding my baby, feeling the warmth of his body wrapped up in the blue bunny rug, gazing at his tiny face and noticing the way he snuggled into me. But at the same time, I could also feel the sunlight that was bathing us both through the windows.

While I fed my baby, I watched kookaburras come in and extract worms from the vegetable garden. I watched rosellas come in to drink from the pond on the 'big rock'. One day I watched two black-faced wallabies as they poked their heads around the mouth of the cave. And then I watched the seasons change. The trunks of the great Angophoras turned to a deep red at the same time as the Jacarandas brought forth their purple flowers. I watched the changing shades of blue on the far hills. I took note of the exact spot the sun set as summer turned to autumn, then autumn turned to winter. I knew the exact tree. I loved it.

Storing up

Then, just eight months later, on Boxing Day 2001, we all watched the bush fire approach. We'd only just finished the back deck in November. At eleven metres by three metres, it was a fairly comprehensive structure. Made purely of timber, it matched the floorboards inside. The indoor and the outdoor spaces now merged perfectly. The kids loved it – they would charge up and down it on their little toy trucks. Then they charged up and down it on their bikes and in-line skates. Then they forgot about the wheels and simply charged.

I loved it as well. For me, it was an ideal space to dream. It was even better in the non-charging moments. Set high over the gully, it provided even better views of the entire landscape. But on Boxing Day it had been finished for a mere two weeks. I don't think we'd even had a proper barbecue on it yet. The electricity wasn't even finished. We had spent every spare moment working on it, but we hadn't quite got around to enjoying it yet.

There are always bushfires in summer in Australia. At that stage, the previous seven years of drought had left most parts of the country a virtual tinderbox. The question became not so much *will* it happen, but *where* will it happen. That particular summer, the fires hit the Blue Mountains pretty badly. We were on evacuation alert from Boxing Day. That meant that all of the photos and pictures were already in the car, ready to go. Actually, the car was so full of photos that there probably wouldn't have been room for us.

The radio was reporting a massive fire front in the Glenbrook Gorge moving directly towards us. The sky had turned into an ominous mix of black ash and deadly crimson. We could even see the flames on the opposite ridge licking up the sky. For about a week our eyes never left the horizon, automatically scanning for the signal that would say 'run'.

The fire had already passed through neighbouring Warrimoo. In Warrimoo, eight houses were lost and still more were damaged. Our friends from church, Lance and Cecily, were among those who lost everything. A wall of flames hit the side of their house which then caught fire. Lance and Cecily were trapped inside the house for ten minutes while they waited for the front to pass by. Then they managed to escape out the front door, with the clothes on their backs . . . and their lives. By the time they reached their footpath, the entire house was up in flames.

The shock must have been dreadful, the realisation of how close it had been. They were overwhelmingly thankful that their lives were spared. They couldn't stop talking about it. They must have grieved their losses, but they were overwhelmingly thankful. Keen musicians, they had lost irreplaceable instruments that had been collected over thirty years of playing. Lance lost his 49 chess sets. Cecily lost her cross-stitches and a quilt that she had put years of work into.

Two and a half years later, in June of 2004, Lance and Cecily came to visit us in Nepal. We spent time going over that particular season. They had rebuilt their house and, in their indefatigable way, carried on as per normal. But losing all your worldly goods has got to change you. It changed them. While we were chatting, we also happened to be busy making nineteen jars of plum jam and storing them up in the cupboard. It was June, the plum season, after all.

But 'storing up' became a recurring theme of our conversation. Lance no longer collects chess sets. Cecily is aware of a strange sensation whenever she makes too many jars of pickles. It's probably not helped by their son Roger. He looks at them with a quizzical eye and says one word, 'Barns'.

Whilst we live here in this richly decorated world, we can't help but take pleasure from all that it offers. We all take delight in making a safe and comfortable home for ourselves. It might look different for each of us, depending on our natures or on the country we find ourselves in, but we still do it. If the opportunity presents itself, it can even develop into a whole season. We knock down a wall . . . or two. We surround ourselves with colours and images that say 'home'. Indeed, there's nothing wrong with that. The colours and images have meaning; they bring comfort and beauty. They bring in the beauty of the world that God gave us to enjoy. Enjoy it, we do.

Perhaps the question is not so much one of sticking to a set of rules. A 'let's never renovate' rule can be fairly inflexible . . . and way too easily broken.

After cheerfully breaking most of our rules, we decided that it might be better for us to look beneath the rules. We tried to remember what was behind the conversation years earlier in Nepal. I think it was the principle beneath the rule. We didn't want anything to enslave us. We didn't want to get so involved in any one thing that it would take us away from the reason God had us on the planet. There must be a level where we can enjoy and revel in the wonderful things that God has given us but the much harder issue is to notice when those things become enslaving. The fine line, if there is one, becomes the faintest wisp of hair. Then, even if we do notice the faintest wisp of hair, it seems to immediately catch the breeze and start floating all over the place. During a season of distraction, it seems to float even more.

For us, on particularly busy days, the renovation did feel enslaving. It seemed to direct the rest of life. We had to check in with the renovation before we checked in with the calendar, let alone with a saner list of priorities. But then, on other days, it didn't feel that way. It felt richly enjoyable. We felt that we could give it up if we had to. Perhaps the more likely answer is that none of us really know. We don't know where the wisp of hair is and we don't know where we sit. Maybe we don't even think about it . . . until the fire approaches.

It's so hard to remember at a moment-by-moment level that the things around us will pass away. They're not eternal. The rich man also struggled. His harvest was so rich one year that he tore down his barns and built bigger and bigger ones. Now he would be OK, he thought, he'd have no more worries. He died that night. In some of his toughest words to the crowds, Jesus says that, in fact, 'this is how it will be for anyone who stores up things for himself but is not rich towards God' (Luke 12:21).

Let's major on our richness towards God. Let's store up for ourselves treasures in heaven, where moth and rust do not destroy and where thieves do not break in and steal. For where our treasure is, there will be our heart also (Matt. 6:21). Let's begin by keeping an eye on our heart.

The fire of 2001 was a probing way to question our heart. At a point where we could have gone either way, God gently reminded us that he was in fact our reason for living. But while we were wondering whether we could give up the house to the fire, a more searching question was already upon us. Now that we had completely renovated our house and turned it into the most ideal location ever to nurture and bring up our young family, could we give it up again? Could we once again turn our backs on all that the West had to offer and return to Nepal? Could we answer God's call to once again serve his people in that Hindu kingdom? They were the same questions: What were we willing to do for him? What were we not willing to do for him? Would the same answers come this time?

14

A SEASON OF CHALLENGE
Blue Mountains, Australia

In many seasons we come up against challenges: unexpected hold-ups, unforeseen demands and temptations, and unexplainable stresses. They meet us head on and we reel beneath the weight of them. This season was not about them.

There was simply one challenge for us – were we willing to return to Nepal? It began on the same morning that Jeremy turned 3 months old. It was June and it was cold, but the recently installed reverse cycle air conditioner was humming away on the living room wall. The fancy new dishwasher was also humming away below the kitchen bench. We were comfortable. We were back in our own, very open, house. We were looking out of the large back windows at the frost on the lawn. The magpies were arriving in order to begin the day's search for food. Christopher and Stephen had already begun their search for food. They were sitting up at the new breakfast bar, enjoying their Weet-Bix and cold milk. Jeremy was having an unheard-of sleep-in. Perhaps at 3 months he was turning the 'small baby' corner?

Our eyes left the tranquil scene in the backyard and we looked at each other. We knew what the question was. But we were less sure about the answer. Could we return to Nepal?

You may be wondering why we were even considering it. Why indeed? Was it not tempting merely to sit back and think, we've done our bit. Maybe somebody else can have a turn now. The thing is, there are enormous needs out there. I'm not really comfortable with thinking, 'I've done my bit.' I'm not sure that Paul ever thought that. He seemed to be too busy thinking 'if only I may finish the race and complete the task the Lord Jesus has given me' (Acts 20:24).

We're all different. The tasks that the Lord gives us are different. To some of us, he gives the task of staying and enabling the work to go on. To others of us, he gives the task of going. Indeed, he gifts us to go. He puts within us a heart for the nations and the abilities to serve him there. And why does he do that? Because his heart is for the nations. It always has been and it always will be.

Many people reminded us of the great needs in Australia. Those needs are significant, but there are also countless people who stay here and are well gifted to meet those needs. They're well adapted to living here and they use their gifts in ways that bring glory to God. They don't necessarily watch aeroplanes flying overhead and wonder about lands and people groups far, far away.

The thing is, Darren and I do wonder about lands far away. It's like God has put Nepal on our hearts and kept it there. In some seasons that means going and in other seasons it means staying and supporting the work from Australia. Maybe that will continue all our lives? At different stages and at different times it will be right to go and at other times it will be right to stay.

In 2001 it seemed like it was right to go back. We were able to. There was no reason not to go. But it wasn't like we had a letter in the mail. I can't really describe how we knew; we just knew. There was no phone call or job advertisement or magazine article or patient in the next cubicle telling us that he knew the only other Australian INFer. We just *knew*.

Sometimes, God leads us very clearly. He seems to say, 'This is the way; walk in it' (Isaiah 30:21). At other times, there's no clear leading. It's as if he says, 'I want you to make a good and godly decision. Based on what you know, based on where you've been, based on your experiences, make a decision that will bring honour to me.'

So we did. We reapplied to return to Nepal with the INF, through the Christian seconding agency, Interserve. But the decision wasn't easy.

Not only were we well settled in our renovated house, we were also well settled in our church and local community. Stephen was ensconced in the local public school and the local soccer club. We had become involved in any number of good things at church, fruitful things: women's groups, outreach events, special services. Darren had carried on meeting with the Nepali group in Sydney on a weekly basis and was busy translating Bible studies into Nepali. Both our jobs had turned out to be quite ideal. We were loving being so close to extended family and friends.

The more settled you are, the harder it is to move. The more you have, the harder it is to give it up. The more people you have to love, the harder it is to leave them. It's an enormous wrench. Even the thought of uprooting our little family, carting them halfway around the world and then replanting in a Third World country was enough to keep us awake at night, many nights. The problem was, we could picture it this time, we could see around the corners. We knew about water problems and electricity problems. We knew how long it takes to readjust and form new friendships in a language and culture which is not your own. We knew about the civil war.

Since 1996, the Maoists had been fighting a civil war in Nepal which had been getting progressively more blood-thirsty as the years went by and their demands weren't met by the government. Since its beginnings 10,000 people had been killed. Riots, bombs and blockades were common. Could we return to a setting such as this? With the boys?

Making sense of something

We began to investigate work options. That's when we started to see the way God works in seasons. He has a plan from the beginning and he will carry it through to completion. The trouble with us is that we plod onwards, not seeing beyond the hedges that border our paths and sometimes not even imagining that there is a path up ahead – certainly not one with a purpose.

While we had been busy completing our family, having major operations and renovating houses, that little physiotherapy course that Darren had helped to set in motion back in 1994 had been busy as well. For the most part, it had sat in government offices, sometimes shifting desks according to the whims of the current bureaucracy. Various expatriate physios had helped to move it along a bit, or helped to change its shape a bit. But as we were ready to return, that same physio training programme had transformed into an accredited three-year certificate course. It was formally accepted into the Dhulikhel Medical Institute, an arm of Kathmandu University. It would begin to take students in August 2002 and INF needed physio tutors from August 2003. That was exactly how long it would take for us to reapply and get back there. Right when we were ready, the work was ready; the work that we had longed for ten years earlier. It must be said: God has a plan.

So often, understanding follows a season rather than precedes it. Darren's brush with death had occurred a year after we came home to Australia permanently. Although we can never see clearly this side of heaven, we came to see 'in part'. If our plans had gone ahead to return to Nepal and do our three-year term in Nepalgunj in 1997, Darren probably wouldn't have lived. In all likelihood, Christopher and Jeremy wouldn't have made it either.

In yet another twist, the government of Nepal brought in a new rule regarding work visas for expatriates. The upper limit was ten years and then you were out. If we had stayed in Nepal, we would have been 'out' before the physio course ever began. We would never have had the opportunity to teach on it, which is what we had wanted to do from the very beginning. But now here we were, available to return and the teaching role was available to walk straight into.

The needs were every bit as dire as they had been ten years earlier. There were now seven Nepali bachelor-level physios for a population of 24 million. The provision of health services in most parts of the country had become worse if anything. The civil war had seen to that. The national church was growing at phenomenal rates but the need for training and encouragement were present more than ever. When more than half of the Christians in the country are less than 5 years old in the faith, some solid teaching doesn't go astray. Although the Nepali church was growing at a phenomenal rate, the percentage of Christians in the country was still less than 2 per cent.

A tree in a hard place

Our two years' leave of absence had long since run out, so the entire application process began again. There were forms to fill out (Do you feel called to Nepal?), interviews (Tell me about your growth in God in the last three months.), CVs (What languages do you speak?), medicals (Is your height/weight ratio within a healthy range?), psychological testing (Tell me about your relationship with your mother), cross-cultural training weeks (In the event of having to hibernate or evacuate, who would take on the difficult decisions?). It seemed to go on for a very long time. But, by the end of 2002, we were officially accepted by both Interserve and INF.

The next step was to again raise the financial and prayer support we would need to keep us in Nepal. Interserve's policy regarding raising support is very upfront. The accepted applicants are encouraged to send letters to all their friends and contacts making their needs known. Two hundred was the suggested target and we wondered vaguely whether we had two hundred friends. More importantly, we wondered whether we were OK about being so upfront.

The policy is based on the image of a steep weathered cliff over a tumultuous ocean. On the very top of the cliff stands a tree. It's a large tree and it leans out over the ocean. In any ordinary environment, that tree wouldn't survive. The buffeting of the waves, the ocean winds, the salt and the spray would all be too much for it. It certainly wouldn't be able to provide shade, green healthy leaves or nourishing fruit. But when the tree is well supported by a large root system that extends into every corner of the cliff, the tree can live. The root system is the support team. From the tiniest rhizome to the largest taproot, the supporters are life itself. Without them, the tree wouldn't stand and it wouldn't hope to thrive. We sent the letters.

Then came the follow-up visits to churches, prayer groups and mission meetings. Once again, we were surrounded by people wanting to know more about mission. They wanted to pray and give and understand more of God's heart for the nations. Again, we felt privileged to catch more of a glimpse into what God was doing in our own country and in our own back yard. It was an inspiring season. It was a season of waiting on God to see how he would provide, not in our timing, but in his; we were thankful for it.

Bravery

But as well as being inspiring, it also raised some recurring questions and statements from the crowd.

'Are you sure about taking the kids?'

'You're crazy. Is it safe?'

'Isn't it a terrible sacrifice? You're throwing away your career and your earning capacity. What about your mortgage?'

'You must be very brave. I couldn't do it.'

Ten years earlier, people had been quite accepting of our decision to live and work in Nepal. They thought it was quite reasonable; after all, that's what many young people do, especially young people without commitments – they go off on adventures.

But people with small children and mortgages generally don't. Well, none of their other neighbours had done it anyway, which meant that there must be something very odd about us.

Actually, the comments on bravery were the ones that got me the most. I would spend hours thinking up helpful responses. 'No, really, I'm not very brave,' I'd say. 'I'm as scared as you are.' Or, 'Maybe we're all brave in different ways. I can't do the things that you're doing. God makes us all differently – he enables us all differently.' But none of our responses really seemed to fit. The bravery comments kept coming.

Then one day we were doing a study on the book of Acts and we were up to chapter 14. Paul and Barnabas had arrived in Iconium and begun speaking in the temples. At first, there was much success and many people believed. But this was soon followed by two bitter waves of persecution, the second involving violence. Paul and Barnabas must have got word of it because they moved on to Lystra and Derbe. Once in Lystra, there was the healing of the man who had been crippled from birth. Then the crowd really went crazy, convinced that their gods from ancient times had come back in human form. So they bowed down before Paul and Barnabas. The sacrifices were already at the city gates. The people were not going to let this opportunity for worship of gods to go unmarked. But Paul was so horrified that he tore his clothes and shouted with all his might: 'Men, why are you doing this? We too are only men, human like you. We are bringing you good news, telling you to turn from these worthless things to the living God, who made heaven and earth and sea and everything in them' (Acts 14:15).

Paul went on to bring the good news to the farmers in a form that they could understand. But again, some Jews stirred up the crowd and this time they managed to find a target for their violence:

> They stoned Paul and dragged him outside the city, thinking he was dead. (Acts 14:19)

If the Jews thought Paul was dead, it says something fairly clear to me. He must have been pretty nearly there. There must have been very little life left in Paul, the stoning had well and truly done its job.

I read the passage and tried to imagine the agony of rocks pelted at my trunk, my face and my arms . . . until I was nearly dead. But while I was still flinching from the onslaught of the rocks, the next sentence quietly got me:

> But after the disciples had gathered around him, he got up and went back into the city. (Acts 14:20)

He got up and went back into the city, the same city in which he'd just been stoned almost to death. Staying in the moment, I tried to imagine it was me. I tried to imagine lifting up my battered and torn body and slowly turning my feet back towards the city, the city which held my attackers. I couldn't of course. There are some things that my imagination just doesn't do. So I looked to the only conclusion available to me. He must have been brave.

But even in my concluding, I wondered whether Paul would have said that he was brave. It's unlikely. Perhaps he would have said instead that he knows who he believes in. He might have said simply that he serves the living God. And if the God we serve is really everything to us, then it's not bravery that leads us on. It's because we know who he is and, deep within us, is a longing to see him honoured in the place we live, wherever that might be – whether it's the ends of the earth or the ends of our street – which, of course, could be the exact same place. We want to show the love of Jesus in the place where he sends us. And we go because we know who he is, not because we know who we are and not because we're brave. We go because he first loved us and put a fire in our souls. 'Love each other as I have loved you,' he said (John 15:12).

Risk taking

Other people said, 'What if something happens to one of you?' It was a fair question. It was not that it hadn't entered our heads. During the season of challenge, it was probably the major thing entering my head. The media were busy reporting some heart-rending stories coming out of Nepal. The Maoists were setting buses alight – full buses according to the media. They were kidnapping young men from villages in 80 per cent of the country. The army was responding in kind. Villages were being plundered, torture and rape were common.

The official INF stance at that time was that these atrocities were happening outside of the main cities and INF was not condoning travel into those areas. In addition, they said that expatriates were not currently being targeted so it was a matter of being well informed and careful. But nobody can guarantee our safety. It's all too easy to be in the wrong place at the wrong time and that can happen in any country. A high-speed traffic accident can maim as well as a bullet from a wayward shot.

Still other people said, 'The safest place of all is at the centre of God's will.' I knew what they were trying to say, but I wasn't sure about the expression. Being in the centre of God's will can't guarantee safety either. Nothing can. How can it? If it's our time to go, it's our time to go. Alternatively, if it's not our time to go, there's nothing on earth that can bring that about. It sounds callous and cold and maybe even a bit simplistic – and we'd all prefer something warm and comforting with some kind of guarantee that would assure our peace and safety.

At times, during the season of challenge, I seemed to desire guarantees so much that I would search Scripture for examples of Gods protection – anything to make me feel better. And it was easy to find the examples. Hebrews 11 was a good one. I happily read the conclusion of the chapter outlining the lives of Gideon, Samson, David and Samuel, the giants of the faith:

> Through faith [they] conquered kingdoms, administered justice, and gained what was promised; [they] shut the mouths of lions, quenched the fury of the flames, and escaped the edge of the sword; [their] weakness was turned to strength; [they] became powerful in battle and routed foreign armies. Women received back their dead, raised to life again. (Heb. 11:33–35a)

It was what I was looking for, my fears and anxieties could take a rest; they could even fade away as I felt secure in the knowledge of God's enabling hand on my life. He will protect us, I thought, he will save us in our time of trial.

But then, of course, I noticed that I was actually right in the middle of verse 35. I hadn't finished reading it. Perhaps I should, I thought, but a glance further down the page revealed a twist in the tale. No, perhaps I shouldn't, I thought. People died. So at that point, I carefully closed my Bible and went back to the kitchen to make some more *dal bhat*. But in the middle of the night, in the quiet and the stillness, it came back to me – unbidden and uncalled for – the rest of verse 35, describing the lives of the giants of the faith.

> Others were tortured and refused to be released, so that they might gain a better resurrection. Some faced jeers and flogging, while still others were chained and put in prison. They were stoned; they were sawn in two; they were put to death by the sword. They went about in sheepskins and goatskins, destitute, persecuted and ill-treated.' (Heb. 11:35b–37)

The unbidden thoughts returned. Maybe being in the centre of God's will only guarantees safety for half of us, not for all of us, I thought. The only tricky thing would be to figure out how I could keep myself forever in the first half, rather than the second. Because no matter how hard I tried, the fear of the second half kept returning. And maybe that's what happens to all of us, over time. Perhaps that's why we've been building our walls higher and higher – till we can hardly see over them. If God is not going to protect us, we think, then we'll have to do it ourselves. So we live our lives in places where the risks are minimal and in a style where the risks are minimal because, after all, what would it say to our kids if they knew we had taken a deliberate risk, and died?

Darren replied calmly. 'It would say to my kids that more than anything else, I'm on this earth to follow Jesus. If following Jesus means taking the hard calls, then that's what I *want* to do. I want my kids to know that I took risks.'

Matthew 25 describes a story about investment. The man called his servants together and delegated responsibilities. To one he gave $5,000, to another $2,000, to a third $1,000. The first and second went to work immediately and doubled their master's investments. The third dug a hole and carefully buried his master's money. It was a very secure hiding place, there was no risk there. But was the master impressed? No.

> It's criminal to live cautiously like that! . . .Take the thousand and give it to the one who risked the most. And get rid of this 'play-it-safe' who won't go out on a limb. Throw him out into utter darkness. (Matt. 25:26–30, The Message)

Those are tough words and they're not ones that you can easily explain to the grandparents. I remember having dinner parties where the subject would come up. We would be grilled about the wisdom of taking our family into a civil war.

'Well, you know, longevity was never really the aim.' It sounds like a fairly flippant response to a serious question. But, actually, we discovered that most people would end up agreeing. Deep down, they agree that life is not about the number of days we spend here on this earth, it's about *the way* we spend those days here on earth. But it's easy to agree at a head level, at a philosophical level. It's much harder to live out, 'how we spend them'.

It was not that we didn't worry. I'm a skilled worrier. In the season of challenge I moved into unprecedented worry levels. I remember the day the security email came from INF. It was reminding members that they should strictly obey all curfews, regardless of whether they were set by the Maoists or the government. In some centres, the curfew was set at sunset, 'Please be aware that if the curfew is broken, the army has been advised to shoot on sight.'

Reading that email in the comfort of our house in the Blue Mountains was difficult. I looked down the hall at our timber front door. It had thick cedar panels and stained glass wild flowers in the top section. I tried to imagine walking out of our front door at the wrong moment and getting shot at. Outside

our front door there was a little porch with an archway, covered with climbing roses. Beyond the archway there was a
winding path of pebbles, bordered on both sides by lavender
and crimson dahlias, and taking us all the way to the picket
fence. Trying to imagine walking out there and being shot at
was impossible. I tried to put the image away . . . whenever I
could.

In whose strength?

Instead, we focused on getting ready. I discovered that it's
harder when there are five of you. There's not only more to do,
but there's more people to think about. I was always wondering what the boys were thinking and how I could prepare
them well for such a major transition.

We still didn't have a confirmed departure date. The
Interserve policy was that at least 80 per cent of our support
costs had to be pledged before the air tickets could be booked.
Well, watching the support pledges come in was probably one
of the most encouraging things I had done in a long while. All
sorts of people came out of the woodwork and gave of what
they had. It was humbling, and then it was humbling again.

But when we reached about 65 per cent, we had a plateau
and it lasted for about three months. It was quite a long three
months. No more pledges were coming in. We tried to look at
it critically. Was this all that we could get? Who else did we
know who would possibly give? We couldn't think of anyone.

So I made myself busy packing, to get my mind off the problem. There was always more packing to be done so I began
sorting through a box at the back of our cupboard which
should have been easy. It was dusty from long years of being
unexplored and if it had been unexplored for that many years,
then it probably meant that I could pop it straight into the stor-

age room under Dennis's house, without any rearranging. I quickly leafed through the contents and came across my journal from our previous years in Nepal.

This could be interesting, I thought to myself. It never hurts to get distracted while packing, so I brushed off the dust and thought I might just look at one page. The page I turned to described God's faithful provision. I'd written, in detail, story after story of the way God had provided for us. At the end I'd concluded that God always provides what we need. Not a cent more, not a cent less, and never a moment early or a moment late.

A few things passed through my mind in that moment: Hmm . . . I used to be wise. How come I'm not wise anymore? I read the stories all over again and started to pray, very humbly. How many times do I try to take back from God the control and the worry – even when I've already learnt the lesson thoroughly in a previous season? It so easily becomes: I can do all things through my strength, not his.

As soon as I finished praying, the phone rang. It was Marion from Interserve. 'You've had two large pledges within the hour,' she said. 'It means that your support has jumped up from 65 per cent to 80 per cent, so I'm going to call the Melbourne office and ask them to book your tickets immediately.'

It was exactly the moment that I prayed. We were on the plane.

Well, almost. There were still another forty-six boxes to store and then four barrels of the most valued things to take with us. That meant teddies and Lego and Mick Inkpen books, not to mention physio texts. Everything else was happily spread around our friends' houses or discarded at a garage sale.

Then there were the weddings. First, Darren's sister was married in her church in the city. A reception by the water gave us ample opportunity to relish the beauty of Sydney's harbour and remind us that we weren't going to be seeing it, or them, for a very long time. Then my brother Tim was married on the edge of a windswept cliff in the Upper Blue Mountains. That was a full two weeks before we hopped on the plane and the reception for 80 was held in a marquee at our house. Didn't I tell you that we could now easily host great crowds of people?

Just to prove it still further, we had 100 friends over for a farewell barbeque the following weekend, on the wonderfully all-purpose deck. The kookaburras kept watch in the gum trees, the hordes of children played continuous games of cricket and explored the caves and the 'big rock'. The adults gathered in amicable groups. Our Nepali friends were welcomed. The blues of the distant hills merged with the friendly hum of conversation. I savoured it and wondered how long it would be till we did it again. All of life takes on a new hue when you're about to leave it behind you.

Our commissioning service had been that morning. The church hall expanded to contain the masses and Graham shared from Ephesians 6:10–18:

> Finally, be strong in the Lord and in his mighty power . . .

It was a good reminder and we needed it. We weren't strong and we weren't brave. Instead, we were weak and scared. But it's only as we cover ourselves in his armour, that we can withstand anything at all. We're only brave in *him* and we're only strong because of *him*.

A time to give up . . .

Then we were sitting in the car, on the way to the airport. We all yelled our goodbyes to our most favourite places as we passed them – the soccer fields, the library, the supermarket, the church, our house. The car sped on down the highway and all that was safe and familiar and comfortable slipped from sight once again out the rear windows. I watched it all slip away and felt the dull ache within me – the one that accompanies letting go, without any reassurance that we would ever pick it up again.

It was another difficult season and one which I'd rather avoid. But I do think there's something good about letting go. As we kept going to the airport, it felt like there was somehow less between me and God as I left behind the familiar things that I'd relied on for years. I needed to find my peace in him rather than in the view from the back deck.

Then all too soon we were walking through Sydney's International Airport terminal once again, looking back tearfully on the assembled crowd and waving. Jeremy was a cuddly 2½-year-old, snuggled in my arms, blissfully unaware. Christopher had just had an 'aeroplane' party for his fourth birthday. It was the beginning of what could well turn into a lifetime's obsession with aeroplanes. Stevie, at 8, was matter-of-fact. He knew that three years was a long time but he was up for the adventure. So were we all.

15

A SEASON OF THANKS
Pokhara, Nepal

The twelve-hour aeroplane trip, with three boys, was still great. But we didn't spend all those hours recovering our emotions. We didn't even bring a book to read or expect to look out the window. The boys got the window seats and they got our entire attention.

A month before the flight, we were speaking at a prayer meeting in Tamworth. The boys were fairly tolerant of our speaking engagements and they were creative in their attempts to amuse themselves. That day it had been a variety of balls in the front garden of our host's house. We actually thought they were doing really well. I'm not quite sure what the supporters were thinking because after the meeting, while I was enjoying the carrot cake, I was tentatively approached by a concerned lady.

'I've been watching your boys for the last two hours,' she said. 'They're quite lively, aren't they! So I've decided I'm only going to pray for one thing for them. I'm going to pray for your aeroplane trip.'

She was quite right to be concerned. Three small boys are a challenge on a long aeroplane trip. If sleep happens for them, you rejoice. You don't even begin to imagine that it will happen for you. But we had a good supply of sticker books, which kept us going for most of the waking hours. The hardest thing was meal time. Our boys love juice so they were delighted when the attendants kept offering it. They kept enjoying it.

That meant that by the time all five meal trays were settled on five small lap trays, their bladders were full to bursting. But how do you get each boy (near the window) out to the toilet whilst balancing all five meal trays on the remaining seat? As soon as you deal with one boy, the next one needs to go. It's the law of the aeroplane. And how do you do it without spilling juice, coffee and Thai rice all down your lap? Then, how do you prevent the rice and coffee from mixing with your honey coated peanuts? I still have no idea, but I do know how gracious Thai attendants are.

By the time we had survived transit at Bangkok we had moved into anticipatory mode. We were nearly there. The old man next to Darren turned out to be a Nepali who was returning from Singapore. He was a wealthy trader and a Buddhist and he wanted to talk solidly about religion. The conversation wasn't anything out of the ordinary, but to us it was the reminder that Nepalis want to talk religion any time they can. They want to put it out there and discuss it. After spending years relearning religious sensitivity in Australia, we would once again have to learn religious freedom in Nepal. Well, make that 'freedom of conversation' anyway.

Flying into Kathmandu in October 2003 wasn't 'relief' as it had been in 1993 or 'awful' as it had been in 1998. In October 2003 it felt like . . . 'home'. We were back home and we'd learnt about the seasons. In the process, we had come full circle.

The snow-covered Himalayas once again spread out to the right and left as far as our eyes could see. All the little houses were once again dotted on every ridge and the rivers were winding their way through the cavernous valleys. The concrete block houses loomed closer as we drew into the chaotic Kathmandu Valley.

'Are the houses going up or coming down?' asked Stephen.

The same green INF vehicle took us through Kathmandu's

busy streets and crowded market areas. The boy's faces were firmly planted against the windowpanes, their eyes growing wider and wider. Bicycles loaded down with baskets of vegetables careered in front of us. A dozen chickens were strung over one man's shoulder. Another carried what looked like at least a hundred crates of eggs. Motor bikes and *tuk tuks* competed for space in a wild unchoreographed dance of the road. Jeremy and Christopher were so busy pointing out new and incredible sights that they didn't have time to complete a sentence before the next one would come. They shouted single words over the noise of the traffic. Somebody had to acknowledge this strange new world they had entered.

Although Nepal was home for us, it was certainly anything but home for the kids. We spent a full week in the INF transit flat in Kathmandu and for the first few days the boys simply refused to go outside. It was far too scary and unfamiliar. So we took it slowly. We stayed inside and watched through the windows. We watched ducks sloshing in the mud (the monsoon was on its way out) and we watched the lady in the flat across the road cleaning her teeth. She was on the third floor and somehow managed to lean all the way out of her window and spit all the way down onto the road. The boys watched her, fascinated, as they dreamed up new spitting possibilities.

We listened to a man noisily clearing his throat and the pigeons calling to each other. We enjoyed the sounds of bicycles heralding their presence with bells. We smelt the incense wafting up from the neighbour's *puja*. We smelt the rice cooking downstairs and heard the unmistakable 'fizz' of pressure cookers going off. It could only mean one thing. We were back in Nepal. By day three, the boys were OK about going out the door.

The possibilities

So we took a vehicle up to Dhulikhel for the day. It was our first sighting of the place that would be home for the next three years. Dhulikhel is a small Newari town about 30 kilometres to the east of Kathmandu. It's the home to the Dhulikhel Medical Institute (DMI), where the physiotherapy course had commenced. The road is by and large 'good'. It has to be because it's the main route to Tibet. Traders regularly use this road to bring supplies in and out of China, as do an infinite number of motorbikes, buses and huffing tractors.

For the first half-hour it was difficult to tell whether we were still in Kathmandu or not. The same blend of concrete buildings and bazaar areas seemed to straggle ever onwards, punctuated by a succession of polluted rivers. Then suddenly the road began to head upwards and we moved out of the smog and the noise and the industry, and into a setting of heavily terraced hills and rice paddies. It was a grand amphitheatre of greenery. Around the edges of the amphitheatre were ridges and on each ridge was a scattering of brown mud dwellings, connecting the scene to the people who lived and toiled there.

We tried to absorb each new scene. It was so amazing to be seeing it for the very first time. There were no memories yet. There were no 'remember whens' or connections between the scene and our lives. It was all brand new. We didn't know where the hospital was, or the church, or the Dhulikhel Medical Institute, or the vegetable lady. We merely saw the possibilities.

Dhulikhel itself lay on one of the ridges. The town seemed to meander along as if there was really no point in coming to a definite stop. Why not keep going? We stared at it all as we passed the shopping bazaar, a police station, a jail, a football field, another school and then, after a while, we came to a more obvious end. The path headed up a forested hill and halfway up there was a house that we had been advised to have a look at. Would it suit us?

It was within a compound of three houses and seemed to be something that would work for us. Downstairs there was an eat-in kitchen and a living area. Upstairs there were three bedrooms but I didn't particularly notice them. I couldn't. I couldn't keep my eyes off the view. From every north-facing window there was a view of the entire Langtang range of the Himalayas. The middle hills seemed to introduce them, gradually taking our eyes ever upward until they met the gleaming white peaks.

We said yes . . . quickly. Views are everything.

The cycle of memories

It was tempting to move in straight away. The planner in me was already picturing the furniture we would need and the curtains I could make. But the season wasn't quite ready. Instead of setting up home, we again hopped on the ten-hour bus to Pokhara for another three-month language block.

We kept commenting on the ten-year cycle. Every bend in the road brought back images of us doing it in the previous decade. But we didn't just rest back and reflect during that bus trip. Every moment of that ten-hour bus trip was taken up with responding to the boys' fascinating observations. It's actually much more fun seeing Nepal through the eyes of your child. You see the rock crackers and the monkeys and the banana trees and the man carrying cauliflowers. You see the gravel maker and the peanut seller and you wonder what it would be like to do that all day long, every day. You don't have time to worry about the landslides or the river 30 metres below you . . . although whether your stomach notices it or not is another issue. At one stage, I did question the wisdom of using our throw-up bag on the remains of Jeremy's smelly nappy.

It's very strange repeating some of your life markers exactly ten years later. We were often struck by our different responses. Ten years had actually changed us. We responded quite differently to issues of poverty. I'd like to say we responded with more wisdom but I'm not entirely sure. Maybe we just saw the complexities more. Things were not quite as black and white as they had been ten years earlier.

Things were not quite as simple either. We learnt that we had to take the boys into account. We didn't live with *Aama* above the buffalo this time or spin buttermilk with a frayed rope. Instead, we house-sat for a Canadian family who were home on leave. It was ever so much easier. Right next door was the INF mission school where the boys joined another twenty expatriate kids for a season of expanding worldviews. They learnt that kids from the Netherlands, Germany, Britain, North America, New Zealand and Nepal all play soccer . . . ferociously.

We relearned our conjugated verb endings. We even learned some new grammatical structures. How come we never knew this before? we asked. My latest theory is that language learning is strongly tied up with personality, with a fair bit of auditory memory and motivation thrown in as well. Darren is an extrovert. He's a quiet extrovert, but he's still an extrovert. His favourite thing is chatting with the taxi driver, the holy man, the fruit lady, the kids by the road . . . actually anyone he can find. His language is quickly integrated into his life, and every new structure or vocabulary list he learns is reinforced immediately. I'm an introvert. These days, if I'm on a bus, I'll chat when I have to and I'll enjoy it but I also quite like to sit and dream. I can spend hours just imagining endless possibilities. I'm still fascinated by people and I love trying to get inside their heads but I don't always go looking for more chatting opportunities. I wait till they come to me. And therein lies the difference. Darren's language is now very impressive. Mine is quite functional. It gets me by.

But being back in Pokhara wasn't all about learning new language structures. It was mostly about our Nepali friends. In the past, I've had people say to me, 'Friendships with Nepalis won't ever be like the friendships you make in the West. They won't be the same depth. They can't be. You can't connect at the same level because your worldviews are just too far apart.'

There's some level of truth here. But maybe every friendship we make is unique? Maybe every friendship we make has a quality that isn't shared with anyone else? What I have shared in one season with one friend will not be repeated in another. Every friend I have has travelled along a unique road with me and shared a unique view on life at that time. Even my close friends in Australia haven't fully understood my years in Nepal. And how can they? They haven't journeyed it with me. There is one friend in Nepal, however, who knows part of me that nobody else ever will, and that is Lalu.

A well to pour

The first weekend we were back in Pokhara, we made the one-hour journey from the top of the Pokhara Valley down to the bottom, to our old church near the little yellow house. We could hear the singing from about 100 metres away. My body started to move in anticipation, to the beat of the Nepali drum. We were almost running.

By then, the membership had grown to about four hundred, and a new church building had replaced the old, in an attempt to accommodate all those extra knees. Mind you, there was still no room to actually let your knees flop into cross-legged sitting. There was still very little room for all the hordes of children. I quickly realised that I had become one of those women with children crawling all over me.

I found Lalu straight away. She was about three rows ahead of me, her hair tied back and her sari folded immaculately. She also seemed to be surrounded by children. I looked again, trying to recognise any of them. But five years is a long time in a child's life. The backs of their heads held no clue. I pondered it all during that three-hour church service.

One of the reasons Lalu and I had become close was that she had shared my season of longing. We had shed tears together while we waited for children. At that time, she already had a 13-year-old daughter by her Hindu husband. But three years of marriage to Saroj hadn't added to her family. She longed to have a baby with Saroj. So we cried and prayed together. During those years, my prayers were seemingly heard and answered. Hers seemingly were not. It's got to be one of the hardest things. Why does God seemingly say yes to one and not the other? I don't know. But I know that it makes it worse. I ached for her. She seemed to have so much love to give. She poured her love on Saroj and Dil Maya but there was a well left within her. On whom could she pour her well?

When I had last seen Lalu in 1998, Saroj was about to begin work with Prison Fellowship. His work took him to some of the most desperate places in the country and he began to see a need for work amongst the prisoners' families. Then after a while he began offering his home to the children of the prisoners who had no other relatives. It started off small – two girls in the gutters who had been left to die. Then, two little boys with severe eye infections. Every time Saroj went off on a trip, he would come home with a small, unwanted child. By the time we were sitting in church again, in 2003, Lalu and Saroj had nine children.

We went to their house for *dal bhat* straight after church and I couldn't take my eyes off Lalu. She was surrounded by children. They were in her arms, at her side, helping her in the kitchen, studiously doing homework. She was beaming. Her prayers had also been answered and her season had turned. She had children to love.

She was beaming, and I had tears in my eyes. I couldn't stop thinking of those years of longing. We don't often get a glimpse into God's long-term plan or see his handiwork. But when we do, we give thanks in new ways. My tears were tears of thanks and not just for the way he'd worked in my friend's life – although that was brilliant – it was also for being given the opportunity to see it. For being able to be back in Pokhara at that exact moment – in time to give thanks.

When we live in one place for most of our lives, memories can get piled up on top of memories – layer upon layer of events and emotions which aren't easily separated. When we walk down the main street of our home town, images come to life but the images can be blurred, merging into one. When did that happen? Who was I with? What was I thinking? It's not always easy to distinguish them.

But our years in Nepal had been punctuated by some fairly significant seasons back in Australia, so the effect seemed to be a heightened awareness of events, images and emotions. When I walked down the lanes of Pokhara again, I saw myself holding Stephen's tiny hand as he learnt to walk in his first pair of squeaky *chappals*. When I sat in Nepali church, I saw myself crying with Lalu. When I ate *dal bhat* with dear friends, I saw where they'd come from. And it caused me to give thanks in ways that maybe I wouldn't have otherwise.

And it seemed to put all of life into a new perspective. A decade on and all of our original group of Nepali friends were thriving. Not in a material sense. They were still living in one-roomed houses with one light bulb. There were a few more hooks on the walls because they had children now. They still couldn't afford the electricity bill. But they were all running the race with joy and completing the tasks the Lord had given them to do. They were working at the Bible correspondence course, for Prison Fellowship, and a Children's Outreach programme. Shankar and Bishnu Maya were putting forty orphans through school. We ate *dal bhat* with each of them and our eyes just kept growing wider as we heard their stories. There was so much to be thankful for.

So, theoretically, we spent those three months in Pokhara learning language and eating *dal bhat*. But more than anything, we were learning about being thankful. We were learning the joy of looking back and seeing the way God works over time. It was even clearer now that we'd come all the way back around the circle.

16

THE SEASON RIGHT NOW
Dhulikhel, Nepal

It can indeed be a joy to look back and see the way God works through seasons. It can bring forth thanksgiving that we didn't know was there. It can even bring understanding that we didn't know was there. We start to see a little bit of the beauty that God has been making over time. The beauty that was so often masked during the seasons as we lived them. For those of us who like to see a glimpse of the path between the hedges it can bring a chance to make sense. A very small amount of sense, at times, but even the small amount seems better than nothing.

The much harder task is to live within the season 'right now'. In my season right now, I'm sitting halfway up our hill on the Dhulikhel ridge. As I've been writing this, July has turned to August. But August in Nepal also means rain. This year's monsoon has seemed endless. It's our seventh . . . or have I already said that? Right now, I'm watching the water pour down in streams across the windowpanes. It's splashing into the mud beneath the swings and making a thudding noise on the roof of the chicken coop. It's bouncing off the banana leaves and landing on the beans below them. Just as inside the house, the boys are bouncing off the walls and landing on their recently constructed Lego castle.

I deal with the casualties and then return my gaze to the view out the window. The black clouds have absorbed the sky, the weight of them seems to defy gravity. Even the mud houses that sit precariously on the ridge opposite us have been blackened into oblivion. My ears pick up the thunder in the distance and it reminds me that the season isn't done yet. The physical seasons don't tend to move on until they're ready to.

A time for war . . .

Neither do the seasons of our lives. We moved to Dhulikhel in January 2004, eighteen months ago. The season hasn't been easy. Thanksgiving hasn't always jumped out at me. Adjusting to living within a civil war has been difficult. The war is by no means the only part of life here, but for us it's the new part.

There's a large army camp about 100 metres down our hill, so we regularly hear gunfire and bombs going off at night. We have been trained to assess whether the gunfire is 'just practise' or something more serious. Is it regular? Is there a pattern to it? Is there a sound like a response? The questions are easy to answer in the daytime but they're a little bit more off-putting at night. There's something about being wakened from your sleep in the dead of night by gunfire, which is not altogether reassuring. The curfew is set at nightfall and I haven't heard of any shootings on sight, but I'm not about to risk going out after dark in order to test the system.

Our house has been assessed for bullet protectiveness in the event of being caught in the crossfire. The downstairs toilet is the only room that has all internal walls and no windows. So guess where we've been told to gather in an emergency? It's about 120 centimetres square, so I'll let you know how we get on if the five of us ever have to sit out a long emergency.

This current season has also been one of limits. Not in a bad way, but limits nonetheless. While Darren has been faithfully teaching the physio students, I've been primarily at home providing schooling for the boys. In Dhulikhel there is no mission school conveniently located right next door.

I am definitely not a primary school teacher, but I have to say that I'm loving it. I really wouldn't exchange this season for anything. I've loved getting inside the boys' heads and discovering more of what's in there. It's shown me their passions and fixations. Stephen has a thing with maps. That means he has a thing with the entire world. He plays capital city games whenever he can. Christopher will analyse and create anything with wings. If I could just draw aeroplanes into every single literacy lesson we would be doing fine. Then again, when we don't find a winged activity, we're struggling. Jeremy will only learn his sounds if the rewards are kisses. Nothing else interests him. Not praise or stickers, not even lollies. Wrestles will do it.

As well as practising our wrestling, we've also been grabbing opportunities to pursue enormous amounts of applied learning. We've taken excursions down to the national parks and been riding on elephants, hunting for wild things. We've trekked the Annapurnas and ridden donkeys through the deepest valley in the world. We've found fossils and eaten Tibetan bread. We've journeyed to the Tibetan border and watched the monkeys in China.

We've also found ourselves in a new Nepali church. It sits on the third floor of an old concrete building. The steps to the top are worn and chipped. You have to watch your step as you climb, as do the chickens that are underfoot. The friends at this church haven't been busy teaching me about worship though. They've been teaching me about peace, and that's because they know about it. They've taught me about a season of peace that can exist right through a civil war.

The stories from this new season are worming their way out, wanting to be told but I can't tell them yet. Just as the monsoon isn't finished yet, this season in Dhulikhel isn't finished either and I can't tell the stories until it is. Why can't I?

I think it's because I don't know how it will end up. I don't know how long it will go on for or what I will make of it in the end. I don't know what I will have learnt or how I will emerge from it. Without the perspective of time, it's very difficult to know. It's very difficult to live in the season right now.

Looking back on the seasons from a distance can be easy. It can even be a blessing. Because the seasons are finished, we can neatly wrap them up and name them and describe what we learnt from our toil. We can even see how it fitted together and how God used it over time. But in the season right now, we can't say those things.

It's tempting for me to want to do that. It's tempting for me to even start writing and to start wondering what I will call this season. Will I call it a season of civil war? Maybe, it's certainly been a feature of this season. Last year, the Maoists announced two major blockades of Kathmandu. The city was under siege and our road was cut off indefinitely. We worried about our food and gas supplies.

Then earlier this year, the king announced a state of emergency and took over the country. All communication was cut, both within the country and with the outside world. We wondered what would come of it. We watched the reactions of the political parties and we waited for a resolution. In August 2005, we're still waiting. Nothing is certain. So perhaps I shall call it a season of civil war.

But, then again, what I've been learning about is peace – the peace that comes from knowing who is reigning. Jean-Pierre de Caussade wrote that, 'Regardless of how things appear at a given moment in time, all of history will ultimately serve to accomplish God's purpose on earth.'

When we live through seasons of war, it's very difficult to see how the things around us could possibly be accomplishing

God's purposes on earth. The things around us appear hideous and that's because they are. Our physio students are telling us how their homes have been blown up. The women at church are telling me of their loved ones being kidnapped. The papers we receive every morning are telling us of murders and torture, rape and pillage. Children are being trained to plant landmines. How is any of this accomplishing God's purposes?

It's very difficult to see. But I'm slowly learning that I don't need to see everything and that even though the things before me are hideous, they're not the full story. They're certainly not the full story to God, who sees everything and who cares and who acts. He is not panicking, he is reigning. In this season I need to work very hard at seeing things through his eyes.

A time for peace . . .

That's what my Nepali friends at church have been busy teaching me. They're teaching me about peace within a setting of civil war and, actually, perhaps the very best place to learn about peace is within a civil war. They know about peace because they know what a lack of peace is like. They even have a word for it. Peace is *shanti* and a lack of peace is *oshanti*. A great many Nepalis in the bazaar these days describe themselves as being *oshanti lagyo* (feeling a lack of peace or unrest). On a wider scale, a lack of peace is a civil war: bombs, strikes, protests, murders. At a personal level, a lack of peace is fear and worry; worry about the next meal, anxiety about passing exams, fearing the abduction of their sons. They know about a lack of peace. They certainly know about it better than I do. So when they first know the touch of God in their lives, the very first thing they speak about is a sense of peace.

Last month, twelve young people were baptised in the local river. They stood by the river and shared their testimonies. Unknowingly and unrehearsed, each one of them described the changes that knowing God had brought to their lives and each one mentioned that it was the *peace* of God that had convinced them of the truth of the gospel. Bowing down to gods of stone had never brought peace like this. Around them, the lack of peace continues, the civil war carries on, the food shortages are still there. But within them, they know peace. They know that *shanti lagyo* comes from God alone and they teach it to me. So perhaps I shall call it a season of peace.

The moments

But then again, I've also been busy learning about a season of limits. In this season, I'm very limited in the things I can do. It's not just that the boys are with me every single minute of the day, it's also the curfew after dark. We're inside every single evening. We try to get home school done in the mornings so that our afternoons are free for outings. Anywhere really: the bazaar, the vegetable lady, the soccer field, the top of the hill to watch the eagles. Anywhere that is 'out'. But the physical seasons have also added to my limits. In the middle of the monsoon, when every afternoon brings a constant drenching rain, getting soaked in the name of adventure hasn't really appealed. So that has neatly ruled out that possibility as well. Cabin fever can be a very real condition, for me as well as them. I'm so limited. It's good that I have learnt in a previous season that 'being' is more important than 'doing'. But there's always room to learn it again.

I can learn, too, that God is not limited and he doesn't have a limited season. He'll do whatever he wants to do around me and within me during this season. In fact, maybe he can only do what he wants to do within me during this season of limits. And I'm beginning to notice the moments too: the twenty children I teach at Sunday school; the monthly meetings back in Kathmandu with Resham and Sita at the Bible correspondence course; my time with the boys; my opportunity to enable Darren.

There's a thought there. Just as we learn best about peace within a civil war or about hope within hopeless or about his adequacies within our own inadequacies, so we also learn best about opportunities within a season of limits. God's plans are beyond limits and we notice it all the more when we're limited. Maybe we don't need to notice it when we're not limited. I never fully realised that until this season. So perhaps I shall call it a season of limits.

And on it goes. Right in the middle of a season, we just don't know. All we can do is live. And in the living, we grow and we learn, we enjoy and we cry, we struggle and we rejoice. We do it right now, without knowing what's around the corner or what will come out of this season.

And that's what I need to learn to do. I need to learn to do my living right now, in the middle of this season, without knowing anything. I need to learn to live in this season, not the next one or the one before or the one I might prefer to be in, but in this one.

So I turn my attention back to the season at hand and move through it, sometimes slowly and sometimes quickly. It feels like a quick one today in Dhulikhel, but tomorrow might be slow. On good days I ask to learn all that I can in the season of the now. I appreciate its peculiar qualities and I know that God will ultimately use it for good, whatever that might look like.

Some friends have shown their concern for me during this season in Dhulikhel. 'Are you sure you're OK up there?' they've said. 'You're quite isolated and you don't have a lot of support. Home school must be hard. Are you going to be all right?'

The answer has evolved over time. 'I'm fine . . . and yes it is hard, but I'm loving it.' And then more importantly, 'It's a season.'

I think the response used to mean, 'It will come to an end.' But over time it's come to mean much more than that. Now I'm starting to think, 'Well, if this is a season right now, what can I learn? How can I grow? What is there to enjoy? What are the most important things for me to do? What is the most important way for me to be?'

It seems that in every season there's a new truth to be learned and it may be a truth that can only be learned in that season. The comfort I experienced during a season of pain wasn't repeated during a season of joy. His voice that I heard during a season of longing was different to the one I heard during a season of distraction. The enabling I am experiencing now during a season of war may not be repeated during a season of peace.

But that's OK. It's a different season. It has a different purpose. We all know that if the seasons were the same, there would be no growth. Without winter there would be no spring and without frosts there would be no bulbs and without the monsoon there would be no rice harvest. In the same way we also know that without sorrow there would be no joy. Without pain there would be no healing. I think that's precisely where the beauty comes in. It comes in through the fruit of the seasons. He has indeed made *everything* beautiful in its time.

Even so, there will always be times when we don't see the beauty. In those seasons we long for heaven even more. We long for a time when we will have unhindered, unbroken intimacy with God. We long for a time when we won't bounce like ping-pong balls, back and forth, from intimacy to distance. In this world, our experience of the seasons, including all the futility and the frustrations, impacts our fellowship with God, but in the world to come, we will know no such impact:

> The throne of God and of the lamb will be in the city, and his servants will serve him. They will see his face, and his name will be on their foreheads. There will be no more night. They will not need the light of a lamp or the light of the sun, for the Lord God will give them light. (Rev. 22:3–5)

We will see his face, every one of us, all of the time, every single moment. Underneath all of our desires and longings is to see the face of God. That's what we've been made for. We've been made with eternity in our hearts and that's what we have to look forward to, and we do, through every season.

Sitting here in the rain, writing this, has also shown me that he's faithful through the seasons. My times are in his hands and he's held all of my other seasons, so he has to be holding this one. No matter how cloudy it may appear, he's holding it. No matter what happens, he's reigning. Even in the confusion and the civil war, the distractions and the joys, the opportunities and the limits, the blessings and the fears, he's not panicking – he's reigning.

And because he's reigning, I don't need to know how the season will turn out. I can live within the season right now and I can enjoy it. I can resist the temptation to start peering around the corner to get a glimpse of the next season. Instead, I can look for the truths that he wants to show me, right now, in this season, in the middle of the rain.

So I look to the rest of this season, my seventh monsoon, and feel ready to receive whatever comes, whatever he has ready for me. Whether it turns out to be a season of trial or a season of plenty, may I be ready to receive it. For I know that every type of season will serve God's design for me. So I hold out my hands in anticipation.

May we all.

GLOSSARY

Aama – mother
Ba – father
Bandh – strike
Bechnu – to sell
Bhetnu – to visit
Bideshi – foreigner
Bijuli – electricity
Birami – patient
Botti – candle
Carom board – a game played with a round puck and a square metre board
Chammal – uncooked rice
Chappals – sandals
Chiya – a sweet milky tea drink
Chungi – many elastic bands formed into a ball
Dal bhat – rice and lentils forming the traditional Nepali meal
Dev nagari – the script which Nepali writing is based on
Doko – a cane basket carried on the back
GP – Green Pastures hospital
INF – International Nepal Fellowship
Jai Masih – Victory to Christ
Kasto – a shawl
Makai – corn
Mitho – tasty
Mukti – salvation

Oshanti – a lack of peace

Patuka – a long piece of cloth that is wrapped around a woman's waist

Potti – bandage

Puja – worship of idols

Punjabi – a long dress and pants worn by women

Sahuji – shopkeeper

Sari – 5 metres of cloth which is wrapped around the body and worn as the national dress

Shanti – peace

Seti Kola – White River

Singh Bahadur – Brave Lion

Tapaiko khutta kumchaunos – please bend your knee

Telugu – the language spoken in Andhra Pradesh, South India

Topi – hat

Tuk tuk – a small three-wheeled vehicle

Ubhinos – please stand up

WRH – Western Regional Hospital

For more information regarding Naomi's writing and speaking ministry, please visit her website www.NaomiReed.Info and join 'My Seventh Monsoon' on Facebook.

Naomi supports the work of the International Nepal Fellowship, a Christian mission serving Nepali people through health and development work. For more information go to www.inf.org

**INTERNATIONAL
NEPAL
FELLOWSHIP**

Coming October 2011

NO ORDINARY VIEW

A season of faith and mission in the Himalayas

Naomi Reed

'The Himalayan view from our back porch was normally breathtaking, but that day I sat there and wondered. Ten years of civil war, a deteriorating health system, an economic crisis and a political stalemate. It was a background of hopelessness for the lives of our Nepali friends and the community that we lived in. In such a setting of pain and darkness, how could God reveal his nature? And how could he call me by name? I wasn't sure. I didn't think it was possible.'

From within the uncertainty of Nepal's civil war, Naomi continues the story of her family's desire to train Nepali physiotherapists and share God's love in word and action. Her honesty and genuine longing to see God's purposes and sovereignty make this unforgettable reading.

978-1-86024-843-6